The Game of
SQUASH

5 Easy Ways to Improve Your Game And Win More Matches

by

GW00602779

James Eth
John North

in 23 Categories in 7 Countries

Copyright

Website: www.thegameofsquash.com
Email: info@thegameofsquash.com

1st Edition 2016

First Published 2016 for John North and James Ethan
by Evolve Global Publishing
PO Box 327 Stanhope Gardens NSW 2768
info@evolveglobalpublishing.com
www.evolveglobalpublishing.com

Book Layout: © 2016 Evolve Global Publishing

ISBN: (Paperback) 978-1-68418-768-3
ISBN: (Hardcover)
ISBN-13: (Createspace)
ISBN-10: (Createspace)
ISBN: (Smashwords)
ASIN: (Amazon Kindle)   B018JXYRE4

This book is available on Barnes & Noble, Kobo, Apple iBooks (digital), Google Books (digital)

Table of Content

About the Authors

James Ethan

James Ethan's story is inspirational to all would-be squash players.

#1 International Best Selling Author and highly ranked world-class squash player, James was by no means a 'natural' when he first tried the game. His first attempt at playing squash began at the age of 17, when his older brother took him down to the local squash courts for a game.

From that very moment James became addicted to the sport. But the skill that he consistently demonstrates today certainly wasn't evident back then.

In those days (the late 80's) the racquets were quite different to how they are today. The size of the head was smaller, and they were heavy and unwieldy because they were made of wood...like holding a sledgehammer!

All of which made the game that much harder to learn. Especially for James. Typical of most new players, he found the game very demanding, and to be honest, he wasn't very good at it. For that reason, no-one wanted to play with him.

Yet he loved playing, and was determined to master the game. Rather than giving up, he continued to practice until he began to improve. After several months of solid practice he was able to take on and even start beating the more experienced players at the club.

By the time he was 22, James achieved 'A' grade status. This achievement encouraged him to play even more squash matches. By the time he was 25, he had achieved state grade level and the game had become his life.

At the state grade level, players are usually either ex-world-ranked or young up-and-comers. For James this meant that he had to contend with a much higher quality game. This drove him to further improve his skills, and he started to train six days a week: running, gym, squash practice and coaching.

By the time he was 30, James was ranked # 250 in the world, which allowed him the opportunity to travel more to locations such as Melbourne and Queensland. He continued to win tournaments along the way and maintain his ranking status.

The next step in his career was to become the manager at Seven Hills Squash Centre in Sydney, and he then went on to manage Northmead and Dural Squash Clubs.

But his personal development and training as an elite squash player didn't end there.

James began to develop his own unique system which helped him build 15 competitions a week. Every night was a different competition and a different style of game.

Most people think there is only one type of squash game but, as James discovered - with some imagination and creativity many exciting variations can be created to keep players interested and motivated.

In 2008 James finally achieved his dream to become the owner of Baulkham Hills Squash & Fitness. Having his own club means James can have his courts operating seven days a week with numerous and varied competitions, to suit all levels and types of players.

And he continues to be an inspiration to us all!

John North

Like most first-time players, John didn't immediately take to the game of squash. He started playing at the age of 15, but hadn't had much experience in the way of ball sports. He honestly believed he'd never get the hang of how to hit that strange little black ball.

He stuck at it because it was so much fun, and within a few short weeks his game had vastly improved, and he wondered how it could have seemed so difficult.

John is a great believer in the fact that anyone can play squash – all you need is some basic coaching. It really doesn't require a lot of skills to have a great workout and have fun at the same time.

At the age of 18, he was lucky enough to be living in a small country town where they decided to build a local squash court. This meant he had an opportunity to try the sport again. John virtually lived at the courts, playing almost every day and constantly improving. The owners let him look after the courts which meant he would play anyone who came along.

This led to his lifelong involvement and commitment to squash, and it continues to be a big part of his life. He has been involved in many of the squash clubs he's played at, and also became Treasurer of the North Queensland Squash Association

The highest ranking John achieved was lower 'A' Grade, but he always had a passion to improve. Even after over 30 years in the sport, John believes there is always room for improvement.

As co-author, John has always had a burning desire to help write a book that could help any player, beginner or advanced, with ideas, and give them strategies to improve their game and win more matches.

Introduction

The Game of Squash Book is written to help beginners to advanced players get more out of their game and find ways to win more matches.

We believe squash can become very addictive but what a wonderful addiction!

Most players strive to improve, but the lack of discipline or knowledge can hold you back.

The Game of Squash is designed to give you an easy resource for all things squash.

The Game of Squash aims to give you a comprehensive look at the game of squash. We will also cover the history of the game, the rules, ideas on how to improve. We also have some featured contributors on nutrition, sports injury prevention, and treatment. As well we have an interview with a player who managed to play on the world squash circuit.

Here are just some of the topics we cover:

- Who can play squash – a description of the game and what you can expect to get out of it
- A basic understanding of the rules
- How to choose the best squash racket for you
- Tips and tricks for improving your game

- Nutrition ideas to improve your health and energy levels
- The importance of injury prevention

If you've ever felt even mildly interested in playing, this is the resource for you. It will tell you absolutely everything you need to know, and hopefully encourage you to make squash a valuable part of your life.

And for those of you who are seasoned players, here's a positive goldmine of secrets to help you take your game to the next level.

We would especially like to thank all our contributors including Brendan Limbrey , Kathy Roorda, Garry Pedersen and Steve Walton.

We hope you enjoy this book!

James Ethan and John North

Chapter One
History and Rules of Squash

History

The game of squash has a cultural and social history rivaling any of the more "old" and traditional sports like rugby. Squash has been played for over 140 years but has grown rapidly in the last forty.

Most people would think that it has tennis as its roots, but it is not some simple variation of tennis or new-fangled idea thought up by tennis players who wanted to add a fast paced and multidimensional aspect to the game. No – squash has a very particular and great back story.

In the year 1148, the French played "la Paume", which meant "the palm of the hand", which was then developed into Jeu de Paume, Real Tennis, Royal Tennis or simply Tennis.

In France, around the twelfth century, many boys and girls played ball games in the narrow streets of towns. They would actually "slap" the ball along the awnings or roofs with the balls bouncing off various structures and even into shop and door openings.

The Rules would change town by town. After a time, these ball games migrated even into the old monasteries. The sound of the ball could be heard slapping back and forth in the courtyard with their gloved hands. The balls were not the spongy, springy rubber globes as they are today.

Monks later added webbing on the gloves, after which they were able to extend their hand by picking up a stick or branch.

By the end of the fifteenth century, the Dutch invented the racquet. This ball game did go on to be called tennis. It did become the national sport of a dozen European nations and then out to the "colonies" (like the USA and Australia).

But the game of hitting a ball with a stub racquet or your hand continued to evolve and change – looking back to those days of the ball bouncing madly and somewhat unpredictably off unusual surfaces.

In 1830, some boys from Harrow School outside London ignited the beginning of squash proper by combining rackets and the hand).

"The Corner", a popular area in the school grounds, was used as a "court" with two side walls and a front wall with a reinforced wall. This street and school grounds game required fast reactions and split-second decisions. The ball went off in all sorts of crazy trajectories which and bounced off drainpipes, chimneys, ledges and window frames.

The Harrow students used a rubber ball which "squashed" against the wall when it was hit. The boys decided to slice off the end grip of their racquets so they could play slower and easier game. They then named it "baby racquets" or "soft racquets". This boys' yard game became a game today which is now called SQUASH.

Squash continued to develop further with changes in court width and length, materials as well as the rules of the game.

Squash in Great Britain started without any real official standards. Great Britain formally created their squash standards in 1923, but squash in America had been played under a different standard for two decades. In the U.S., squash courts were built in universities, clubs, and even at home.

Squash Tennis USA style is one of the few racquets and ball indoor sports that can be termed strictly "American" in origin (whereas Squash Racquets has its roots in England).

The game spread to America in the 1880s and the first real organized Squash Racquets play in the USA was in 1882 at St. Paul's Prep School, in Concord, New Hampshire.

Over time in the, USA, an exciting offspring was born called "Squash Tennis."

In the last decade of the 1800s saw two Squash games being played. However, Squash Tennis became more popular and widely played in the USA over Squash Racquets because of a more exciting pace and action of the play.

As well several private courts were constructed on estates owned by such millionaires as William C. Whitney and J. P. Morgan.

The Tuxedo Club, in New York, constructed the first official Club court in 1898. By 1905, the Racquet and Tennis Club, Harvard, Princeton, and Columbia Clubs in Manhattan had courts, as did Brooklyn's Crescent.

The onset of World War II saw the death squash ball because of the shortage of rubber. At the same time, Squash Racquets thrived during the War.

Competitions were established at service bases, colleges, schools which mean a new breed of young, active Americans became addicted to Squash Racquets. Even the Titanic had a squash court in 1912.

As the 20th century drew to an end, professional Squash was still dominated by countries like England, Australia, and Canada.

A new player arrived on the scene as well, Ahmed Barada from Egypt joined the ranks. On the women's front, the WISPA rankings were still dominated by England, Australia, and New Zealand. Sarah Fitz-Gerald, Carol Owens, Cassie Jackman and Leilani Joyce (Rorani) were regular ranked players,

Men's squash in Egypt and France came forward and by 2009 Amr Shabana, Ramy Ashour, and Karim Darwish where the top of the list for Egypt. In the women's rankings, new talent emerged with Malaysia's Nicol David and Vanessa Atkinson of Netherlands, the Grinham sisters from Australia and Natalie Grainger of USA.

Squash and the Olympic Games

Squash made its first bid to be included in the Olympics in Barcelona Games in 1992 and Atlanta in 1996, Sydney in 2000, Athens in 2004 and Beijing in 2008.

A formal bid process was put in place for selection for the 2012 Games; Five sports, including Squash, were selected, but Squash failed to secure the two-thirds majority necessary.

For the 2016 games, Squash lost again to to golf and Rugby7s.

The bid process is underway for the 2020 Olympic Games, with one place available and squash Squash is poised to gain its overdue admission to the most prestigious event in world sport.

Globally there is an estimated 50,000+ squash courts in 185 countries. England had the greatest number at 8,500. There are an estimated 20 million squash players worldwide.

This history shows that squash has evolved like most sports into a global game of speed and thrilling action. Yes, it is true that looking back to the old days it was a game of young boys.

In the 1970s and 1980s, teenage boys would play squash typically on a Saturday morning.

But for the future of squash to be bright, we need to get that excitement back for the youngsters again and as the community realize more and more through education - movement is vital for a long and healthy life.

Attracting young players is one of the keys to the future of squash as a game for a broad spectrum of players - in both age and gender.

Rules

The aim of this chapter is to give you a basic understanding of the rules of squash. It's not intended to be a comprehensive guide. There will be links at the end if you want to know more.

Now tennis has a beautiful simplicity in its rules and scoring. Sometimes we wonder if the casual observer of squash gets the wrong opinion of the game's complexity due to its seemingly frantic pace and loud gameplay.

Because squash has both players close to each other as opposed to tennis, many of the rules are in place to protect from injury. The biggest piece of advice any player can take is that "when in doubt call a let". Which means if you think you may cause injury to your opponent or feel they are close to you, simply stop and call "let". This pauses the game play while a referee will make a decision whether to play the rally again or award a point to the let caller.

These rules apply even when you are playing a friendly game. It never ceases to surprise us that players at any level can cause injuries when they should have called a "let".

Squash rules are pretty straightforward and with a short period of practice very easy to master.

So let's get started...

First, the winner of the toss gets to choose which side they want to serve from and alternates sides until they lose a point. The toss is typically done by spinning the racket, with one player guessing whether the racket will land up or down based on the direction of the logo at the end of the grip.

Typically, you will start your serve from the right side assuming your opponent is right handed. Most players are weaker on the back hand. However if they are left handed you would start from the left side.

The ball can hit any number of walls (i.e., sidewall, back wall) but must eventually hit the front wall before bouncing on the floor. A rally (the exchange of shots) ends when one of the following occurs:

- The ball bounces twice
- The ball hits the tin
- The ball is hit outside the lines (or on the lines)
- Interference resulting in a stroke or let.

The serve is done by having at least one foot in the service box, then hitting the ball to the front wall, above the service line and having it bounce in the opposite quarter-court. The receiver can stand anywhere on their box as long as they do not interfere with the server. Only one serve is allowed. There is no second serve as in tennis.

Your opponent has the option of volleying return your serve before it hits the ground. After hitting the front wall first, the ball may hit any other number of walls before landing in the opponent's quarter court. However, a serve is illegal if it hits any sidewall before hitting the front wall!

Following the serve, the ball can hit any number of sidewalls before hitting the front wall.

The red lines mark the out of bounds of the court. So all shots must be below the lines. If the ball touches the line, it is considered out!

Scoring is to 15 with a point-a-rally (PAR), where every rally is a point, regardless of who served. So if you serve and lose the rally, then your opponents get a point and gets to serve.

Usually it is the best of five games, If the score reaches 14 all, the game will be won by two clear points (which will be expressed as 13-11).

You also have traditional English scoring to 9 points, where only the server can win a point. This means if you serve the ball and lose the point, then your opponent gets to serve and the score does not change. If you win the point, then you get a point and get to serve from the next side. When service changes, it is often called 'hand-out'. When hand-out you can pick which side to serve from, after which you alternate sides if you continue to win points. The first player who gets to 8-8 chooses 9 or 10, called set 1 or 2.

The 11 point scoring is the official scoring for world squash.
Some not-so-obvious rules of squash are you cannot carry the ball or hit the ball twice, but you can make several attempts at striking the ball as long as only contact is made once.

Detailed rules

If you would like more specific rules and regulations you can look at:

Abbreviated version of the World Singles Squash Rules to help players to understand the basics:

http://www.squashsite.co.uk/abbreviated_rules.htm

Official website of the world Squash Federation, including official rulebook:

http://www.worldsquash.org

Squash Australia official regulation website:

http://www.squash.org.au/sqaus/regulations_policies/regulations.htm

Squash rules for beginners:

http://www.buzzle.com/articles/squash-rules-for-beginners.html

Court Safety

Safety is a matter of really being aware of your place in the court and not being foolish. Some people don't mean to hurt you, but they are not paying attention to their surroundings.

Being safe is also about good sportsmanship. If you have got any idea that you might clip the person or hit them with a ball, you just call a let. It's the safest approach and the person's happy to play another game when it comes to them being hit with the second fastest ball in the world.

It's better to call a let rather than get hit by the ball or hurt someone. It does hurt, no doubt about it - it leaves you a sting,

Please call a let if there're any signs of them cramping you or being too close within your swing. Call a let and you'll still get another chance of winning that point.

The Let is really the number ONE rule of squash, and here it is formally:

At any time during a rally a player should not strike the ball if there is a danger of hitting the opponent with the ball or racket. In such cases, play stops and the rally is either played again (a "Let") or opponent is penalized (a "Stroke). (The Rules of Squash, 2001, Rule 8: Rallies)
As you watch a lot of players who are inexperienced, they will try and hit everything and are uncoordinated.

For all players being safe is a primary rule of the game. If you are going to play a risky shot, make sure you have plenty of room to play that shot. It's a must.

If you are a new player, make sure you fully understand that you don't have to be mercenary about hitting that ball - yes it is exciting to whack something as hard as you can.

New players are at a higher risk of causing injuries against their opponent because they tend to swing wider, so they have less control.

If you are playing squash doubles we always recommend wearing protective eye wear simply because there's four on the court at once;

If you take a wider swing than you should, you have a higher chance of hitting of the three other players The glasses are designed to protect your eyes and face.

In fact often, it's a good idea to wear protective glasses even when playing singles matches.

Chapter Two
Future of Squash

Where is Squash Going- A Personal Perspective

Squash has become a neglected sport in recent years with huge marketing budgets that golf and tennis have, Squash has struggled to gain community attention.

The facilities to host squash matches are expensive to build and maintain and many existing squash courts take up valuable and prime real estate positions which end up being sold off for apartments or commercial developments.

The future of squash here in Sydney and globally continues to be deeply challenged to grow and attract new players into the sport.

For starters what Squash needs are keen operators to work together to get four or five clubs together for inner club competitions and special events.

In addition, because of people's busy lifestyles, it is often hard to get players to participate in pennant style competitions which typically requires travel and additional costs.

Every night, Squash clubs need to have some activity or competition operating. Creating and promoting different types of games and catering for all skill levels is paramount to keep players engaged.

Using handicaps and time-based games also means every player has a chance to win even against a stronger opponent.

During the day, a Squash club should try to have something for everyone including mothers and children. During the day for most clubs is empty court time. It's a good idea to encourage mothers and their children to come in during the day. They can play for an hour or so in a group environment with a cup of tea afterwards.

Squash overseas has always been more successful due to, their marketing strategy, and the weather. Because the weather is a lot more inconsistent in Australia, we have a lot of sunshine and a lot of beaches. This has a dramatic effect on indoor sports like Squash.

The Squash Federation has continuously tried to get the sport included in the Olympics. They have a current bid for the 2020 Olympics. It honestly should have been in there as one of the new sports in 2008 or 2012.

Luckily we did have squash as a part of the Commonwealth Games and the sport does really well as a serious part of the games for competitors and spectators alike. But the real key to getting a big kick for this sport is still getting into the Olympics.

Squash will continue to survive and grow in some countries. But it competes with big name sports with huge marketing budgets. Squash is one of the few family sports, where everyone can play and be involved in a local club.

As an existing squash player consider it your duty to find new players and encourage them to try this fantastic sport.

Chapter Three
Squash Basics

Who Can Play Squash?

Anyone who enjoys playing Tennis, or any racket game and has good reflexes will love Squash.

Where squash offers the exhilaration inherent in powerfully hit strokes, split-second racket work, and graceful, seemingly unhurried footwork. The ball "comes to you" more often, but the challenge is to figure out the wider angles and exactly where the lightning fast green ball will eventually end up after rebounding off as many as five walls.

The game of Squash has something to offer players of all ages. The demands for fast reflexes, agile racket work, and speed of foot are intriguing challenges for the youngsters.

On the other hand, placement, guile, patience, and the faster ball that actually provides more time for retrieval, make Squash the ideal sport for the "older" athlete who wants to preserve that straight waistline all of his or her life.

And let's not forget this — for those who think it is a game of fast athletic young men, well, the average age of the ranking players today is around 43! That doesn't mean I am advocating we only encourage middle-aged men to play!

Also, the promising young (10 to 13-year-old) tennis "comer," who cannot play tennis during the winter months and still needs the strength or coordination to hit the Squash ball hard, prolonged, enjoyable squash rallies is an excellent prospect and training addition for their tennis game.

Because the ball is not affected by temperature you can play Squash all year round, and not only in the cold, winter months.

Because of the speed of the ball, Squash is an excellent game for active people of all ages. If you are looking for a sport that you can "master" in one or two seasons it may take a little longer but regular practice will ensure entertaining and fun experiences.

But if you are looking for an intriguing and invigorating game which you can play all your life practically, we strongly urge you to try Squash. You, your waistline, legs, lungs and reflexes will never regret it.

Choosing a Club

When first looking to join a squash club, we suggest visiting a few in your local area and see which one might suit you the best.

Introduce yourself to the manager and try to get a feel for what's happening in the club's general activities and competitions.

Think about and take note of the communication with the manager and any other staff.

Just like in most organizations whether it be a workplace or shop or service industry - the "boss" or owner often sets the tone and quality of the club.

Don't feel shy or intimidated by all the business and noise if it is peak hour at the club.

Take a look at their website, check their competition or notice boards if they've got them. They normally have clippings and boards, and so it's a great way to see how active they are.

Take a look at the facilities, the condition of the entry and the common areas and bathrooms. But then try to get a feel for the human element.

Ask to check a couple of courts to make sure there are no holes in the walls or major damage in the court area.

Is it clean and looking fresh?

In many clubs, the average player plays for around five years. You might also want to look on the walls for sponsorships, newsletters, maybe even a trophy display and there you can check out whether the club is active and successful at the competition level.

Did you get a good feeling from them?

Did they answer your questions well?

What is your overall impression of the club?

What sort of competitions do they offer?

What levels of skills required? eg. do they cater for the beginner or advanced players (depending on your requirements)

What times are the courts open?

What is their regular court and competition charges?

Do the players seem friendly?

Do they offer coaching?

What's the parking like? If you go during the day - go at night as well.

Often the club will have pretty clear signs if it looks after their players and has a commitment to the game and culture.

Choosing a Racquet

The best place to buy a new racket is from your local squash court.

Most courts will allow you to have a small hit with the racket you might like. But be extra careful not to damage the racket, if you do be prepared to buy it!

The weight is the first choice you need to make. A heavier racket rarely works for anybody. Around 150 grams or lighter is usually the best option. The racket weights now go down to 110. But you need to be comfortable with the weight versus your skill and strength,

There are two types of racket throat which are referred to as open or teardrop and closed. Open throat squash rackets have a larger stringbed area, a larger sweet spot and therefore tend to be more forgiving.

Closed throat squash rackets have a smaller stringbed and sweet spot and as a general rule will, therefore, suit a more experienced player.

The lighter a racket, the greater control and feel you get when playing a shot.

Technology has moved fast in the squash world, with the lighter rackets using more sophisticated materials which can produce the same degree of power as a few of the heavier rackets, with better feel and control.

A fantastic combination you may think, but this comes at a cost, inexperienced players may not even spot the difference. So consider these ideas when you purchase your first racket.

The feel of a racket will also rely on its balance point, through the root of the handle. For example, if you will need to balance your racket using your finger between your racket head and handle. It is normally shown in centimeters. The lighter the top, the less power you obtain from the shot and more control and maneuverability. That is just another consideration when looking for that perfect racket that meets your style and manner of play.

Prices for new rackets can vary. For a good racket, there might only be a $10-$20 difference. At the end of the day all rackets can break. They're made to break in a fashion.

So a player has got to be comfortable with the weight and the balance. There is usually a broad range of colours to suit every personality or gender. But at the end of the day, you need to be comfortable and confident with your new racket. It's important to note that it can take up to six weeks to get used to a new racket.

What about the racket strings?

Around three-quarters of strings on a new racket are usually not good quality. They work on racket quality before string quality and rib quality.

So the question begs - Should you budget to restring your new racket?

Yes, some players do. It may seem a more advanced idea but as you play more and get exposed to players of greater experience you start to also to want the best your equipment you can get.

Being one of the parts of the game you can prepare for good quality strings are most important. This change can make a big difference on a racket. It is a bit like getting a better engine in your car. Once you find a racket and you get use to it and really enjoy using it - having a restring does prolong the life of that racket, and it prolongs the investment in it of course as well. So it's a win all round.

What are the different types of squash balls?

Squash has several ball choices, while they all just seem to be a black ball there are many types designed for different games.

The professional ball, the slowest ball is a double yellow dot ball. That's the one that the professionals use. That's the one if you walked on a court and the balls were cold, and you dropped it, it wouldn't bounce very high.

The professionals can hit the ball hard which the ball hot and travels very fast.

The next ball that bounces a little bit more is the single yellow dot ball.

They're really the only two balls that are used in all normal competitions, the double yellow and the single.

Then there's a whole variety of beginner balls. The blue dot is still the same in size as the double yellow and the single yellow, but it bounces the most out of all the balls.

Then one of the great developments has been oversized balls now with thinner rubber.

This is a terrific ball from Grays for school programs or complete beginners.

It's still black and a little bit bigger than a normal squash ball, but the kids don't tend to notice it as much.

SQUASH BALLS

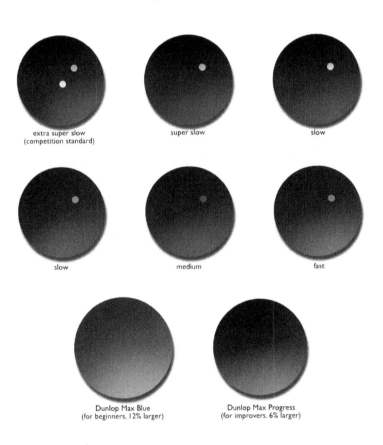

extra super slow
(competition standard)

super slow

slow

slow

medium

fast

Dunlop Max Blue
(for beginners, 12% larger)

Dunlop Max Progress
(for improvers, 6% larger)

Types of Squash Games

There are many types of squash games, like tennis, there are single or double matches. But there are many other variations you may not have known about and can expand experience in the game.

Single Matches include:

- Standard rules first player to 9 or 15 points to wins the game (best of 3 or 5 games)
- Timed for example 10 or 15 mins each, repeated once or twice. Every point counts and the highest score wins.
- Handicapped matches to give a weaker player a chance to win and challenge a stronger player to play harder.
- Round robin style matches where you might play several players one after each other.

Doubles or Other Styles

- "Killer" where 1 player plays against 2 other players
- Doubles matches with various ways of scoring.

How Does Squash Doubles work?

Squash doubles were invented in Philadelphia in 1907 and typically uses the same courts as single matches. Doubles is an exciting and entertaining variation of Squash.

With four players on the court at once, virtually no shot is a winning one and can improve your reactions for a singles game.

Doubles are more of a tactical game, and that can be very appealing to to players.

How's it scored?

Doubles can be scored in a number of different ways.

Play best of fives. Up to 30 points. You can make different scoring thresholds for something different. Three lots of 30 points can go for about an hour and a half. That is one heck of a workout!

Doubles is very unlike singles games where you can just cross court every time, because depending on the other players position you could be playing straight into your opponents hands. With Doubles you need to play a lot more of straight shots along the wall.

What is a traditional game of squash?

A traditional game is best of five to 15. It's been at 15 since 2000 in Australia. Whoever wins three games wins the match. Every point counts.

How do the SquashMatrix.com games work?

The Squash Matrix is an Australia web based system developed to improve the method of ranking of players. The system is based on a player versus player approach.

It's a great way to get a guide of a player's level of skill and ranking against his peers.

How can I relate my new squash matrix number to the old ranking system?

For example, C-grade is 120 to 150 on the matrix. B-grade is 150 to 190. A-grade would be 190 to 250.

How do you score points?

You can gain a maximum of six points in a match. If a 150 player beats a 220 player three-nil, they definitely get six points. So a nice step up the ladder.

It doesn't matter what the score was. 17-15, 15-13. They'll get six points, and I'll boost them. Conversely - the 220 player will lose six points!

Whatever the winner gains, the loser will lose. So it can get very competitive and is a great way to track your progress and to motivate for improvement.

If you play someone that's higher than you and you get a game off them, you still get points. You get half a point to a point. Because on a ranking, you're not expected to win, so it's a bonus if you get a game, if not a match. The opposing player will not lose any points.

If you lose to a similar player, it comes down to how many games you lose.

Chapter Four

Preventing and Treating Injuries

Featured Contributor - Brendan Limbrey

Brendan Limbrey

APA Sports Physiotherapist*BMedSc, BBus, MPhysio, MSportsPhysio

Brendan is a Physiotherapist with a passion for working with patients to provide solutions to their presenting conditions. He applies the current evidence-based practice to assess accurately and offer optimal treatment options. His specific areas of interest are sports and musculoskeletal injuries, orthopaedic rehabilitation, injury prevention and optimising sporting performance.

Brendan has undertaken additional specialised training having completed his Masters of Sports Physiotherapy at La Trobe University, Level 3 Sports Physiotherapy Course, Level 1 Spinal Physiotherapy Course, Level 1 Shoulder Physiotherapy Course as well as training in Pilates and Casting.

As a physiotherapist, Brendan has worked in numerous private clinics and hospitals across Australia, providing him with experience in a vast array of clinical scenarios. He has held various physiotherapy appointments with sporting teams and has experience working with NSW Netball, Holroyd-Parramatta Australian Football Club, UTS Australian Football Club and UTS Soccer Club.

Brendan is an accredited member of the Australian Physiotherapy Association, Sports Physiotherapy Association, and Sports Medicine Australia. Brendan is actively involved with the Australian Physiotherapy Association as a Branch Councillor on the NSW Branch Council as well as being on the Sports Physiotherapy Association committee.

Brendan established Arrow Physiotherapy in Castle Hill in 2012. As someone who grew up in the Castle Hill area, he is pleased to be now operating a business in the local area.

When he is not in the clinic Brendan enjoys spending time with his young family, running, cycling and watching football (since he has now hung up the boots!).

Contact Brendan

📞 02 8850 7770

🌐 www.arrowphysiotherapy.com.au

Brendan Limbrey

Overview

Squash is a sport played at a rapid pace which involves high impact, short, sharp movements with lots of change of direction. These features result in large forces being applied to the leg joints, muscles, and ligaments, which can ultimately lead to sudden injury.

Additionally, repetitive swift and reaching movements of the arm (especially the dominant arm) can lead to the possibility to overuse injuries. The most common injuries in squash players involve the ankles, knees, and lower back.

Preparing to play

Before playing squash, it is important to prepare your body for the proceeding activity, by conducting a thorough warm-up. This is important to help prevent sustaining an injury, and it can also be useful to optimise performance.

An ideal warm-up will gradually increase your heart rate and gradually introduce movements that will be performed during the activity which allows your joints, muscles, ligaments and tendons to become accustomed to the stresses being applied to them.

An example of an appropriate warm-up would include jogging on the spot, forwards, backwards and sideways jogging, carioca movements (often referred to as Grapevine), squats, lunge walking, moving your arms through full range of motion (circles).

And then gradually hitting ball on court initially with minimal movement across court and then increasing amount of movement across court and speed of hitting ball to slowly work up to near game play intensity. Warm-ups can vary in length, depending on the type and intensity of activity being prepared for. The more intense the exercise, the more thorough the warm-up should be. As a rough guide, warm-ups should last between 10 and 20 minutes.

You will notice that the above example does not include any static stretching exercises. Static stretches have not been shown to reduce the risk of injury or prepare the body for exercise. Gradual dynamic movements are superior in their ability to reduce injury risk and prepare the body for activity. N.B. If you have specifically been advised to completed static stretches by a health professional due to a particular injury or foreseen vulnerability that you make have, then you should complete these as part of your warm-up.

Post-activity cool down

At the conclusion of squash activity, it is advisable to conduct a cool down routine to limit post-exercise soreness and aid recovery. A cool down should gradually return the body to its normal resting state. Examples of cool down activities include gentle jogging which progresses on to walking, high knee walking, slow shallow lunge walking, slow arm circles and gentle back bends forward and backward.

Static stretches are more appropriate to conduct in a cool down, although they are not essential. Should you wish to conduct static stretching, stretches should be held for at least 20 seconds and ideally repeated at least twice. Muscle groups that are worthy of stretching include calves, hamstrings, quadriceps, gluteals and muscles around the shoulders and neck.

A cool down routine does not need to be as lengthy as a warm-up. The general principle of the longer and more intense the exercise completed, the longer the cool down period should be. A cool down should last a minimum of 5 minutes.

Injuries specific to squash

There are some injuries which are prevalent among squash players. These injuries are as follows:

- **Contact injuries** – these are perhaps the most common injury sustained on the squash court. With players running around on a court at high speed, swinging racquets and being surrounded by solid walls (made of concrete or glass) and a solid floor to fall on, this lends itself to the possibility of sustaining a contact injury by being bumped, knocked over, stuck with a racquet, falling to the floor or running or pushed into a wall. These injuries can range from the more common mild bumps and bruises through to more severe injuries like fractures or even concussion (should contact be made with the head).

- **Ankle sprains** – the requirement for rapid change of direction and lunging movements can result in a player twisting or rolling their ankle which in turn can damage the ligaments in the ankle, which is known as an ankle sprain. Ankle sprains can vary in severity from mild through to severe. It is common for players to attempt to continue playing with a mildly sprained ankle or even to strap or brace their ankle to allow them to do this. Playing with a sprained ankle is not recommended. In doing so, you risk further injury to your ankle. Ankle sprains have a tendency to becoming a recurrent problem, with many athletes re-spraining an ankle following an initial injury. It is essential that you consult a health professional to establish the severity of the injury and complete a rehabilitation program which will likely focus on restoring ankle movement, strength and balance.

- **Achilles tendinopathy** – injuries to the Achilles' tendon are nearly always an overuse injury or more specifically an inability to tolerate changes in activity load. The exceptions to this are those who sustain an Achilles tendon rupture, in which the Achilles tendon effectively snaps leaving a gap between to two ends. A tendon rupture requires surgery to re-attach the two ends. Once an Achilles' tendon is injured, they can continue to be troublesome if the load is continued not to be managed well and other underlying factors are not addressed. As a general rule, the longer you have had the injury, the longer it tends to take to recover fully. Tendon injuries can be somewhat deceptive in that they any pain tends actually to improve with activity. Even if this does happen, typically the pain will intensify by the next day and is often accompanied by a feeling of stiffness in the region. If you do experience Achilles tendon pain, it is highly recommended that you seek professional advice to help you manage this.

- **Calf muscle strains** – the constant changing of direction and rapid acceleration movements of squash places great demands on the calf muscles every time that you push off your toes, especially in an explosive manner. This situation can result in calf muscle strains (often referred to as tears). Calf muscles strains result in pain in the back of the calf muscle, difficulty and pain rising on to your toes and often discomfort when walking (especially if you try to stride out). Factors contributing to calf strains include muscle strength and endurance, ankle flexibility and fatigue. If you have sustained a calf strain, an important component of the rehabilitation is a graded return to running and explosive movements. This is often done too hastily and can result in re-injury.

- **Knee ligament injuries** – the changing direction, lunging and twisting motions required to play squash can result in forces in which ligaments in and around the knee can be injured. Depending on which of the ligaments in the knee are injured, this can result in different movements troubling the injured athlete. If either of the collateral ligaments (which run down the inside (medial) and outside (lateral) of the knee) is injured, this can result in issues with sideways and pivoting motions. If either the anterior or posterior cruciate ligaments (which sit deeper in the knee) are injured, this can create a situation of instability whereby the knee may give way at times. It is extremely important to have any knee ligament injuries accurately diagnosed and rehabilitated completely before return to playing squash. It is not uncommon for those having sustained serious knee ligament injuries to have some ongoing symptoms of pain or instability. In these cases, it may be appropriate to look at bracing and strapping options for your knee upon return to sport. Consult with your sports physiotherapist for further advice.

- **Meniscal injuries** – between the thigh and shin bones of the knee rests the meniscal tissue, which acts to cushion the knee and absorbs force. It is possible to injure or create a tear in this tissue especially with sharp twisting movements of the knee. It is also a tissue that becomes more susceptible to damage with age. Meniscal injuries can cause people to have issues with knee swelling, pain, difficulty squatting, running and twisting. Depending on the severity of any injury may result in different treatment requirements. Large proportions of meniscal injuries can be appropriately managed conservatively with physiotherapy and medications, although it is not uncommon for more severe injuries to require arthroscopic surgery to address the issue. In either case, it is incredibly important to restore full function to the knee before returning to playing squash.

- **Patellofemoral pain** – a very common type of knee pain is patellofemoral pain, which in essence relates to pain arising in and around the knee cap. People with this issue will often have issues with squatting, kneeling, running and negotiating stairs. This pain can be caused by numerous factors including having a knee cap that sits or is pulled towards the outside of the knee, poor hip or thigh muscle strength, overuse, tight thigh, hamstring or calf muscles, feet that excessively pronate (roll in), inadequate training, poor choice of footwear and the presence of arthritic changes behind the knee cap. Treatment for Patellofemoral pain involves addressing the factors above that are contributing to the condition. It is also common for those with this condition to use bracing or taping (often a strip of tape across the front of the knee) to allow greater amounts of pain-free motion to play a sport.

- **Shoulder injuries** – the repetitive reaching and hitting of the ball can result in some shoulder injuries, which are usually overuse in nature. The rotator cuff tendons in the shoulder are required to work hard to perform this work, and it is not uncommon for these to be subjected to repeated microtrauma which ultimately leads to pain or damage to the tendons. The positions that the shoulder is often repeatedly placed in to play shots can result in certain tissues within the shoulder to become pinched between the bones of the shoulder. This is referred to as shoulder impingement. The treatment of these shoulder conditions varies depending on exactly what damage you may have done and the factors contributing to this issue. One thing is for sure with most shoulder conditions, is if you continue to ignore the pain and continue playing you will more than likely make the injury worse.

- **Tennis Elbow** – pain on the outside of the elbow is commonly referred to as Tennis elbow. The more correct name for this condition is lateral epicondylalgia. It is nearly always an overuse condition affecting the tendons that attach to the outside of the elbow. Whilst the pain is felt at the elbow, it usually has more to do with wrist function as the muscles that attach to these tendons control wrist and finger movements. Factors leading to this injury can include overuse, upper limb technique issues including grip tightness, changes in training load and racquet changes including grip, weight, and size. Treatment of Tennis Elbow largely involves managing the stress applied to injured area, settling symptoms and most importantly improving the load tolerance of the tendons on the outside of the elbow before returning to playing squash.

- **Low back pain** – the lower back of squash players is susceptible to injury due to reaching, bending and stretching movements required to play squash. All of these movements place stress on the lower back. There are many structures in the lower back which can be a source of pain and also many factors which can contribute to developing low back pain. If you do experience low back pain, it is important to consult with a health professional who is experienced in treating low back pain, especially in athletic populations. Treatment options range from manual therapy, stretching, cortisone injections, medications, stretching and strengthening of your core muscles.

- **Eye injuries** – it is possible to sustain a contact injury to the eye while playing squash, especially if you do not wear eye protection (i.e. glasses). The speed of the game and that of which the ball moves, together with the fact the squash ball can fit within the space of the eye socket, opens up the possibility of obtaining an injury by a ball coming in direct contact with your eye. The damage that can be done by a ball coming in direct contact with your eye can be significant. The best way to avoid eye injury is to wear protective glasses while you play to prevent a ball hitting your eye in the first place. If you do sustain an eye injury, you should consult with an optometrist or medical practitioner as a matter of urgency.

Other considerations

Beyond the injuries already mentioned, there are some additional medical conditions to be aware of whilst playing squash:

- **Dehydration / heat stroke** – the combination of inadequate fluid intake, intense exercise and heat can lead to a dehydrated state which can ultimately lead to heat stroke if continuing to exercise in these conditions. The best way to avoid a dehydrated state is to keep up adequate fluids. Symptoms of dehydration include, but are not limited to, dizziness, fatigue, disorientation, headache and muscle cramping. If you experience these symptoms, it is essential that you cease activity, slowly replace fluids and rest in a cool area. If these symptoms persist, it is important that you consult with a medical practitioner.

- **Concussion** – the nature of squash lends itself to the possibility of sustaining a contact injury to the head. Any contact injury to the head has the possibility of resulting in concussion. Symptoms of concussion range enormously from headache, dizziness, disorientation and nausea to loss of consciousness. Concussion is a serious injury and anyone having sustained a concussion needs to consult with a medical practitioner and will need to gain clearance as to when they can return to sporting activities.

- **Cardiac events** – squash, like most forms of physical activity, places increased demand on the heart. This increased demand on the heart can result in cardiac injury. Symptoms can include tightness in the chest, chest and/or arm pain, shortness of breath and loss of consciousness. These events are a medical emergency and the individual involved needs access to medical services urgently.

What to do if you sustain an injury?

If you are unfortunately enough to sustain an injury whilst playing squash, the following guidelines should be adhered to:

Do no HARM which is an acronym which stands for:

- **Heat** – you should avoid applying heat to any newly injured body part.

- **Alcohol** – you should avoid consuming any alcohol if you have sustained an injury.
- **Running** – you should cease activity to avoid making the injury worse.
- **Massage** – unless under the advice of a health practitioner, you should avoid massaging any newly injured area.

You should apply the RICE principle:

- **Rest** – you should immediately cease any activity and rest the injured body part.
- **Ice** – you should apply ice (or cold through other means) to the injured region. As a rough guide, ice should not be applied for longer than 20 minutes at a time. Ice should also not be applied directly to the skin as it is possible to obtain an ice burn.
- **Compression** – you should apply compression to the injured body region. This can be done by applying a compressive bandage over the injured site.
- **Elevation** – you should elevate the injured body region above the level of your heart.

If you have sustained an injury, you should consult with a health professional to have any injury assessed and determine the appropriate treatment for your injury.

Which health professional should I see?

- If there has been significant trauma and you are in considerable pain, then you should present to your local hospital emergency department;

- For most other squash related injuries, the most appropriate health professional to assess you injury would be a sports physiotherapist.
- You could also consider presenting to your general practitioner.
- Should you require specialist medical opinion, your physiotherapist or doctor may make referral arrangements to see a sports physician, orthopaedic surgeon or other specialist.

With the majority of injuries sustained whilst playing squash it is important to ensure that you fully rehabilitate the injury.

It is common for many injuries to become a recurrent problem if they are not fully rehabilitated or to increase your likelihood of sustaining another injury. You should look to be assessed by a health professional before returning to squash or other sport.

In most instances, a gradual return to activity is required.

How to decrease your risk of injury while playing squash

There are some factors that can help reduce your risk of sustaining an injury while playing squash. These factors can be divided into internal and external factors. Internal factors are all those things within an individual that can be adjusted to alter the risk of injury. External factors relate to all elements outside of an individual that affect injury risk.

Internal factors that can reduce injury risk include:

- Improved general fitness – higher levels of fitness allow you to move more easily and proficiently around the court and not fatigue as quickly.
- Improved conditioning for demands of squash – a body which is well prepared for the specific demands of squash and has had the opportunity to develop and practise these movements and skills is less likely to be injured.
- Ensure adequate training load – insufficient training can result in an underprepared body whilst overtraining can place you at risk of overuse injuries.
- Partake in appropriate training activities – training activities should be specific to your level of fitness, ability, and competition.

- Improve technique with running, lunging, changing direction and hitting ball – improved body positioning and technique will reduce the stress on your joints, muscles, and ligaments and may likely also assist your performance.
- Have any existing injuries treated and rehabilitated appropriately – injuries left untreated can become a hindrance due to niggles, residual movement or strength deficits or compensatory movement patterns in effort to not place stress on certain body regions (this can often happen subconsciously)
- If you are unaccustomed to exercise, consult with your general practitioner to seek clearance before commencing any exercise regime.
- If you are new to squash, the speed and movements required can be extremely demanding. It is recommended to build up skills and fitness with slower racquet sports (e.g. racquetball).

External factors that can assist with injury risk reductions include:

- Ensuring courts are in good condition and have adequate lighting.
- Do not leave any items within the playing areas of the court so that they can be a trip hazard.
- Keep courts closed during play.
- Ensure that there are no pools of water or sweat on the court, to prevent slipping over.
- Avoid playing in extreme heat or humidity, which can lead to dehydration, heat stroke, and fatigue issues.
- Use a ball appropriate to the level of participants – squash balls can vary in their speed and bounce qualities, making different balls more appropriate to different levels of ability.
- Ensure adequate fluid intake before, during and after training or playing to prevent dehydration.
- Wear appropriately clothing – clothing should be appropriate for the conditions in which you are training or playing.
- Keep racquets in good condition.
- Footwear – wear well-fitting shoes appropriate for court use which takes into consideration your foot characteristics. If you need advice regarding footwear consult with a sports podiatrist, physiotherapy or good sports shoe retailer.
- Eye protection – glasses are recommended to prevent contact eye injuries, especially from squash balls which unfortunately can easily fit in the eye socket and make direct contact with the eye.

- Using supportive braces or prophylactic strapping tape – there are numerous braces on the market to provide stability and support to most body regions including knees and ankles. Strapping tape can also be used to help prevent joint sprains among other injuries. For advice on whether braces or strapping would be appropriate for your circumstances, consult with your sports physiotherapist.

Tips for those wanting to go the extra mile to prevent injury or improve performance

What can you do if you want to go the extra distance to avoid injury on the squash court? Perhaps you want the edge on your competition and want to recover quicker or improve your performance. If so, the following are worth considering:

- Work with a coach to formulate training plans, train in a structured way, keep you on track with your goals, assess the technical aspects of your game and work on improving these areas.
- Put in place a training diary. This includes documenting what training/game activities you plan to complete and comparing this to what you actually do. This is a valuable tool to help ensure that have an appropriate training load (balancing doing enough vs ensuring you do not overtrain) and including the right balance of training activities in your overall training. A training diary can be established in conjunction with a coach. If you do happen to sustain an injury, looking back at a training diary can be very beneficial for health professionals to identify whether you may have been overtraining or whether certain components of your training may have contributed to your injury. If you have had injuries in the past, especially if they were overuse in nature, it may be worth gaining the input from a sports physiotherapist or exercise physiologist to assist with developing your training diary.
- Get a sports-specific musculoskeletal screening done. This involves consulting with a sports physiotherapist, who has a strong understanding of the requirements of squash, to conduct a range of screening tests (predominantly assessing how well your body moves, posture and strength) as well as taking into consideration any past injuries, your training/playing volume and level of competition to establish whether there are particular injuries that you may be at risk of developing and whether there are any areas (e.g. core stability or strength around your knee) that you would

benefit from addressing in your training to help you avoid these injuries. The sports physiotherapist will likely be in a position to guide you as to what to implement to address anything that arises from the screening. Put simply; a screening helps to identify any underlying issues before a problem potentially arises.

- Work on your strength and conditioning with an exercise physiologist or personal trainer, familiar with the demands of squash.
- Consult a sports dietician to assess your diet with respect to the nutritional requirements of your activity levels as well as taking into consideration individual factors to assist with fuelling your body appropriately for training and competition as well as aiding physical recovery.
- If you are looking for the mental edge then working with sports psychologist might be the answer to assist with developing successful performance routines, preparing for upcoming events, overcoming barriers to success or dealing with issues relating to injury struggles, burnout, concentration, anxiety or controlling emotions.

5 Easy Steps to Improve

Steps to Improvement

One of the key elements for improvement in any sport is your level of enjoyment. If you are enjoying playing matches, you will always want to get to their next level.

Tracking your previous results and improving your fitness is what you need to do to boost your performance.

At least once a week try to play with someone better than you. This will help your overall fitness level and game skill.

Consider having a squash lesson once every few weeks and then keep practicing what you have been taught.

Learning to keep your shoulders to the side, improving your footwork and skills with that racket is a great way to get better at any level.

While years ago footwork was one the main goals in coaching; it isn't as important anymore. Footwork just has to be balanced.

Make sure you keep your racket up ready for the next swing.

Make sure you are focusing on the correct swing technique with your weight forward.

The squash forehand swing is part of a fluent movement technique similar to a side arm throw used to skim a stone across a pond.

The squash backhand swing can be described as throwing a frisbee except that you need to keep the wrist firm.

Whenever you play a ball, no matter if it's a serve to a forehand drive, make sure their weight is forward. Then Follow through. Once they finish connection and swing, move backward to the T as soon as possible (The T is the centre area of the squash court)

The quicker you can move back, the better the chance you will have to hit a great shot for the next ball.

The Squash ball is the second fastest ball in the world, which means it travels fast from a novice player to a ranked player. With ball's traveling that fast your reactions need to be quick as you can.

Focusing on your reaction times is a great way to improve your skill levels.

When serving the squash ball is always going to be the "lob".

It doesn't matter if you're a lower level or a higher level, the lob is still a safety net. The hammering of the ball on the serve doesn't typically work well. With some players, hitting the ball hard on the serve after a game or two they will have expanded a lot of energy. Just a lob serve is very safe and difficult for your opponent to hit, and it gives you more time to get back to the T.

One of the "chess style strategies" of Squash is everything is to do with creating time for you and taking the opponent's time away.

Make sure that the serve is firstly connected to the front wall, maybe even a few centimeters to the other side. But as long as the lob's up high and it goes into the back corner. That will put that's the pressure right there on them. They're forced to volley.
Try to hit the ball long or along the wall first. Hitting the ball long first helps you to control your swing better and hitting good length.

Then when you're feeling more confident, you can play some volley drops and play the ball short. Just remember if your opponent is fit make sure you get to the T ready for the next shot because anything short is still "gettable".

Never turn your body. Just your head. Just enough to keep balance and still watch the ball. That's another way of improving your game.

Here is a couple of great exercises you can do to self-practice when you have 30 minutes or more by yourself on the court.

Start with practicing serving the ball from the forehand to the backhand, retrieving back with a drive, then two drives after that, and then across the court with correct shoulders footwork positioning.

Then, on that other side, which is a forehand, do three drives in a row, and then finish on a cross court.

This exercise is good self-playing straight routine to do; it gives good ball control, and you get to practice footwork, shoulders to the side, and of course the correct timing of the ball.

A coaching exercise to try. Stand in the middle of the court, which is the T, and the coach boasts the ball, a nice soft boast to make it move like an L-shape position to make sure they hit the ball down there with shoulders to the side.

You then just hit the ball at half-pace, so the ball travels nice and tight down the wall, and then the coach, if he's able enough, get the ball back down the wall. Every exercise should be a practice of the game.

Another area to focus on is "serve and return" of the ball.
It's very important because no matter even if you're an A grader or a State graded player, people get quite lazy with their returns, and just hit the ball down the wall to get the game back into play.

Another way to practice is with three players on a court, the coach and two students, and just have them on each side, and get them to hit a ball on each side, get them to hit down the wall, and the coach has to cut the ball off, and just get a few drop shots, and get them to move correctly.

Anything to do with moving, like a game, is the idea of becoming a better squash player.

There are things like just two-on-one games, which means somebody is versing with two people up to 11 or 12 points. It's a great routine where they force off to boast, and they force off to cross court. They've got to play straight, they've got to play tight, and even if one of the players miss it, the other player is backing him up for the shot.

So, get started today. Book a time with your local club and start practicing. Ask around to find another player who is looking to improve and try to schedule the time each week to keep to a consistent practice time.

Preparation

Getting ready for a game of squash is very important. It's not enough to just warm up in the gym. A warm up will just make sure you are limber and warm. Going on cold can affect your muscles even your whole body.
The research is now conclusive that stretching first before you are warmed up can cause more injuries.

Try jogging on the spot or a minute on a still bike. The idea is to break a sweat and get your muscles working and your heart rate up.

You should stretch after you finish your match. Your muscles have been used, over-used even, and you've got to make sure that you stretch well so your muscles aren't so sore the next day.

What sorts of stretches?

After your match stretch your hamstrings, quads and arms as well as your shoulder blades.

Demands of the Sport

Because of its continuous activity, squash is a sport that demands a high level of aerobic fitness. In a typical game, you will be working at about 80% of your maximum heart rate.

Although the distance traveled in each movement is short and explosive, the continuous nature of the rallies with recovery periods in between means that the energy supply comes from aerobic systems. Muscular strength is important for the game and strong legs will aid your anaerobic fitness, while strong arms, chest, and back will help with racket speed and power. Good flexibility is central not only to a match performance but also in helping avoid injury.

The training week

Playing squash at a higher level carries such an extensive range of fitness requirements, and the best-prepared players will have a diverse training program. The amount of the sessions will change throughout the year. To advance aerobic endurance, it is best to do some "steady state" activity. Cycling and swimming will help to condition the heart and lungs, but remember that you play squash on your feet! So naturally running is a good choice.

Court sprints are also a beneficial way to increase anaerobic stamina. This sort of activity does not have to be done on a court; short sprints can be conducted almost anywhere with sprints over 30 to 60 meters.

Work in the gym, lifting weights or circuit training, is an outstanding way to increase strength and should be slotted into your training if possible. In the meantime, do not forget to stretch before and after all sessions, to prepare for and recover from exercise, although dedicated flexibility sessions are useful if time allows.

Game Strategy

Strategy sometimes, with a game - well it's going to depend on a number of factors. If you've never played someone before, you're going to have to wait until after the first game, because you're going to get to know their style and habits.

What you can look out for is if they move to the ball well off the T. If they struggle, if they are not moving correctly to the left-hand side. If they're slow off the mark, if they're huffing and puffing after their first game, then you think you're testing their fitness. And certainly if they're not watching the ball, that's a big thing. If they're hitting a ball and looking at the front wall, there's a good chance you can get them.

The strategy of hitting the ball long is keeping the ball as deep as you can and forcing them to hit loose. A good player can hit the ball deep back again and again. So can you, you hope. You want to make sure, even after about 10-12 drives each, that you create a chance for them if the ball's short or loose, that you create something under pressure.

The concept of people cross-courting a lot, well...any shot is good at the right time. A cross-court will never be good when the person's at the T and their cross-court's a bit short. They take one step, and you're doing all the running. You've got to make sure the person has put their weight forward on one side.

Then you can create that chance of cross-courting to the other side and throw them off balance.

Technically they should be behind you, not in front of you when you crosscourt.

Technically they should be behind you very much in fact. But if you know that they've taken a step to the forehand side, and you've got a chance to cross-court to the backhand, that means you're going to take an extra step, plus their own step to get that cross-court back.

That's the idea. It's all court craft and strategy. Once you get to a certain level, you've got to have court craft and strategy. Normally after the first game, you can find out, their weaknesses or their strengths and you'll know what to play.

Some people don't pay attention to what's going on around them, so they don't have any idea of changing their game strategy.

The strategy in Squash is basically the same as Squash rackets; i.e., to control the so-called "T" or the intersection of the service court lines, by keeping your opponent up front, off to the sides, or behind you, the majority of the time (see fig. 2).

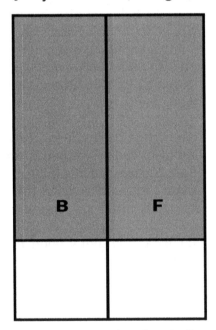

Fig. 1   Note extension of service line to front wall

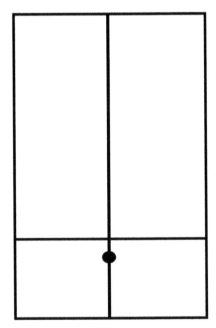

Fig. 2   Desired court position.

The fundamental stratagem can only be carried out by your learning a wide assortment of Squash shots and perfecting your repertoire with practice and experience against many different types of opponents under competitive situations.

You will have to fight and play hard for this position. Always head for the "T" immediately after hitting the ball, but taking care not to interfere with your opponent's stroke. All of your shots should be hit with a purpose, which is to keep your opponent off balance, away from the "T," and of course, eventually to defeat him.

Change of pace, therefore, is of utmost importance. Break up your opponent's rhythm, never allow him to get grooved, frequently do the unexpected, so that he loses confidence in his anticipation and, subsequently, goes on the defensive.

At all times be offensive. The game of Squash has known many so-called "great getters," but they invariably have succumbed to "purposeful power" and the aggressively angled shots of players with the burning desire to win, "the killer instinct" that spurs the great players to go all out for every point.

Play each point like an individual match

Don't let up or intentionally "throw" a game. Squash, as with all racket games, is a sport of momentum. Many a tide has changed, many a match won when seemingly it has been hopelessly lost. Go after every point as though you were down Match Point and had to win it. "Coasting" shatters your concentration, and lost concentration can well mean a lost match. Play to win as quickly as you can.

Finally, assume your opponent will retrieve even your best shots. Don't underestimate his ability or overestimate your shot-making prowess. Remember the speed of the ball actually gives your opponent more time to get to it. Always be ready for anything until the ball is actually ruled dead and the rally has ended.

Fitness for Squash

It's an old saying but "don't play squash to get fit, get fit to play squash."

So exercise and training out of the court will help improve your fitness and performance on the court.

For example interval workouts on the oval as well as longer distance running up to 5km.

When it comes to fitness, you need to choose something they would like to do. If there's a choice they have between, for example, swimming, biking, running, then make a decision. But you've got to be quite fit before you get on that court to play a hard and competitive match.

Stephen Coppinger, winner of this year's South African Squash Champs and ranked thirty-fifth internationally says this: "It involves a complete set of fitness skills including speed off the mark, endurance, strength and stability," and "The intensity of the game means it's a great workout, and it can all be over in about 45 minutes," explains Coppinger.

Squash is a moderate to high-intensity exercise. Players are active 50% to 70% of the playing time. 80% of the time, the ball is in play 10 seconds or less.

Now importantly from not just a fitness perspective but a medical one as well is that the heart rate increases rapidly in the first minutes of play and remains at approximately 160 beats/min for the whole match no matter what levels the players are.

However, the heart rates of players have been known to go right up the age-related maximums (220 - age = predicted maximal heart rate). So even before we think about fitness you do need to be sure your cardiovascular health is suitable for the game. It goes without saying that a game rated as "high" in effort should not be jumped into by people with heart conditions.

So with those facts out of the way - what might be some good fitness aspects to help with your game. Well as it is a game of speed, coordination and stamina you need to incorporate those factors. I would suggest interval training in the gym if you can or make your own routine in a park or at the beach.

A good idea should be to exercise at 75-85% max heart rate. This interval training should be in bursts around 35-40 seconds each as well as around 90-110 seconds with some resting in between.

Interval training will improve your cardio health and stamina while the combination of explosive and strength work will assist in the developing your physical capacities. A combination of sprints, jumps, push-ups, balance work and core strength conditioning will not only assist you in your game - but really - those workouts have been shown to be age beating and help with metabolic health.

Some players do just turn up for their game every week and get a great workout. But I ask you, how many well performing and improving and champion athletes just turn up once a week for a race or a game? None. Now being young you might get away with patchy fitness.

But as you get older, a game like squash will stress parts of your body, and you better be prepared Or you will suffer an injury which is both unpleasant of course but also very frustrating.

Take a look at your schedule and factor in some extra training time and you will be rewarded at match time!

Shot Making

Most people might believe Squash offers nothing but prolonged "slam bang" rallies which you might see as a boring "sameness."

Because of the tremendous liveliness of the ball and the apparent absence of deftly placed straight "drops" that die in a corner, these potential players scorn and speak disparagingly of the wonderful game of Squash, which, like all racket games, has its own shots and ways of putting the ball away.

It is very true that overwhelming power is a key to hitting winning shots, but this is also true of Tennis. Employing the so-called "Big Game of Tennis" is an absolute must if a circuit player today is going to be a winner. No longer do you see any classic baseline duels where the premium is on guile and steadiness. The Big Service, the powerful rapier-like follow-up volley or overhead smash are the standard weapons that pay off in today's Tennis game.

The following are some of the fundamental shots you should attempt to include in your repertoire:

Rails

Your "bread and butter" shots, are the "rails" or shots hit straight up and down, parallel to the side wall. These rails keep your opponents "scrambling" and allow you to hold that important "T" position.

The rail shot is hit more effectually when you are fairly close, within three feet of the side wall.

The closer your position to the side wall, the easier it is to hit a shot that stays right next to the wall during the entire flight of the shot (see fig. 9).

Many winners are made off of these rail shots in the following manner:

1. Frequently the ball hits straight into a rear corner and dies; or
2. It pops unexpectedly out of the corner and right into your opponent;
3. When hit with the proper pace, and low, the ball will die before it comes off the back wall;
4. When hit with sheer power and relatively high, your opponent will be unable to catch up with it;
5. If the ball is hit in such a manner as to make it cling to the side wall all the way back, your opponent will err in attempting to pick it off the side wall.

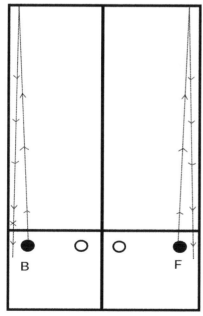

Fig. 9 Straight up and down backhand and forehand rail shots.

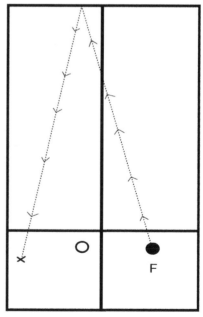

Fig. 10 Cross court to opponent's
backhand.

Cross-courts

To be mixed in with your straight up and down strokes are the cross-court forehand and backhand shots. Here again, these are employed to keep the ball out of the middle and keep your opponent defensive and on the move. They can be hit either straight toward the opposite back wall corner frequently for a winner, or more sharply cross-court, so that the ball either breaks into or behind your opponent's position (see fig 11)

Three-wall Fadeaway

This shot can only be executed when you are a few feet (.5 metre) in front of the service line and off to one side of the court or the other, nearer to the side wall than the center. Otherwise, it is practically impossible to obtain the necessary angle to pull off the three-wall fadeaway successfully.

The ball is hit as sharply as possible into the opposite corner, at a position approximately midway between the floor and the ceiling, striking the front wall first and then the side wall. This particular stroke is hit higher than most of the other Squash shots since the ball has so far to travel.

It will shoot off the side wall at great velocity and traverse cross court, bounce, and hit the other side wall deep—ideally within two feet of the back wall. Then, instead of coming off at the same angle as it hits, the ball rebounds practically parallel to the back wall (see fig. 12).

A well hit three-way fadeaway, which can be made either off the backhand or the forehand, is practically irretrievable since your opponent, even when he comes to realize how the ball is going to skid out straight at him, will still have great difficulty in getting his racket head behind the ball (and in front of the back wall) to make a return.

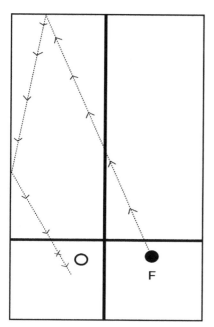

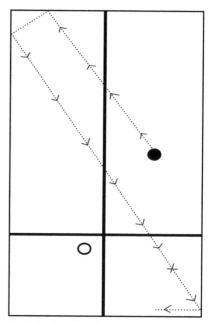

Fig. 11 Cross court that breaks into or behind opponent.

Fig. 12 3 wall fadeaway.

Double Boast

This shot, while not as effective as in Squash rackets, can, nonetheless, result in many winning points or, if not producing a winner, it will force your opponent to the front of the court in order to make his retrieval. The double boast is hit almost straight into the side wall and fairly low (three to four feet above the floor) and can be hit either off the forehand or backhand side.

The ball rebounds off the side wall, goes cross court and hits the opposite side wall just inches away from the front wall. It bounces out and practically parallel to the front, barely touching or "kissing" the front wall for a winner, or at least a very difficult "get" for your opponent (see figs. 13 & 14). The only prerequisite for hitting this shot properly is that you should be fairly far back in the court and close to one of the side walls before the execution of your shot.

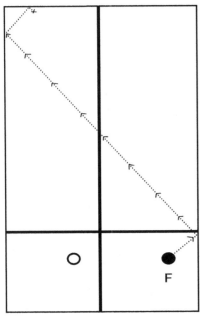

Fig. 13 Forehand boast.

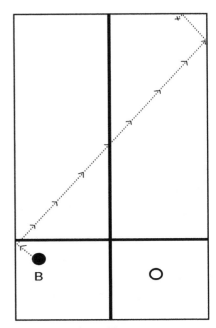

Fig. 14 Backhand boast.

Four-Wall Boast

This particular shot is much more difficult to master than the double boast or three-wall fadeaway but, at the same time, far more effective and unexpected. It has to be hit with a good deal of power and quite high to carry to the front wall. Your chances of success are, therefore, far greater if attempted off the forehand side.

The ball travels off your racket high into the backhand or left wall, rebounds sharply to the opposite or forehand wall heading toward the front of the court. There should still be enough momentum and height remaining to permit the ball to again go cross-court to the left wall where it hits within a few inches of the front wall and drops straight down barely, touching or "kissing" the front wall (see fig. 15).

The four-wall boast is presently only hit by a handful of the better Squash players and should be a shot you attempt only after becoming skillful in the other more standard winning shots.

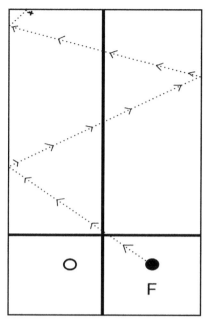

Fig. 15 Fourwall boast.

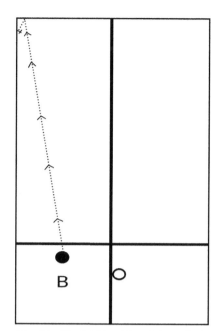

Fig. 16 Straight backhand drop shot.

Straight Up and Down and Cross-Court Drops

These soft or "touch" shots are employed primarily to move your opponent up and back, although an occasional winner will result when a low ball, hit with the right amount of pace and spin, dies before your opponent can get to it.

Too few Squash players today, including many of the ranking competitors, employ this change of pace shot. Of all the shots, this one must be hit with a short, low follow-through in order to work successfully. Your primary goal to accomplish these shots is to make certain you hit the front wall first and, ideally, not allow the ball to angle into the side walls (see figs. 16 & 17).

Corner Shots

Again, unlike Squash rackets, the Squash corner shots rarely result in an outright winner. The ball is just too lively. These shots are worth employing occasionally, however, to keep your opponent cross-legged, off-balance, and on the run. The most effective corner shots are hit with fairly good pace.

Your aim should be low and into the side wall to a point much closer to the front wall than the spot a Squash rackets player employs. The reason for hitting a corner shot in this "in and out" manner is to keep the livelier ball out of the center of the court (see figs. 18 & 19).

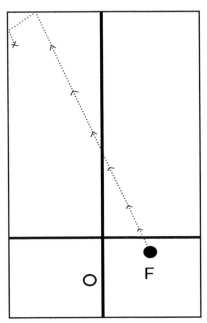

Fig. 17 Cross court forehand drop shot.

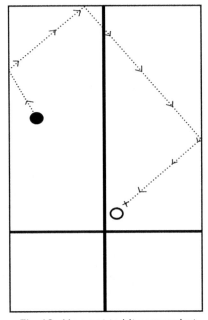

Fig. 18 How not to hit corner shot.

Miscellaneous

It is best when hitting any Squash shot to "hold" your shot as long as you can, thus reducing the chances that your opponent can anticipate where you are going to put the ball and start moving to position even prior to your actually hitting.

Whenever possible, shield the ball with your body so that your opponent cannot see the direction you have hit until the very last possible instant. There is nothing in the Playing Rules against blocking your opponent's view, as long as you do not interfere with his swing or with his getting into the proper position.

Remember that the key to your shot making is mixing up your strokes and keeping the ball angled away from the middle of the court. A ball that ends up in the center will probably result in your losing the point or, at best, having to leave the "T" and go on the defensive. The exception, of course, is the widely employed "gut ball" that you hit into the front wall with great speed and at such a height that it rebounds right into your opponent's body (see fig. 20).

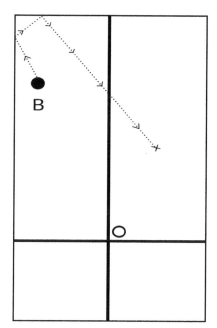

Fig. 19   How to hit corner shot.

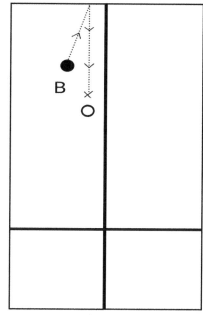

Fig. 20   Ball aimed to rebound off front wall and into opponent.

Employ the side walls as much as possible to keep the ball ricocheting and rocketing about the court, so your opponent becomes frustrated and almost dizzy from following the flight of your angled shots.

Turning

A word on "turning" or "coming around" is in order. In Squash, it is both required and desirable to come around as frequently as possible. The Squash ball is so lively and the angles so wide that trying to back up usually results in the ball chasing you and at best, a defensive, awkward shot will be all you can hit. Turning, however, and moving constantly after or toward the ball will "open up the court" as well as place you in a solid, firm position to stroke the ball freely and comfortably.(See Figures 21 and 22 showing a player backing up versus a player who is properly turning.)

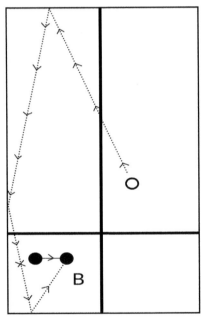

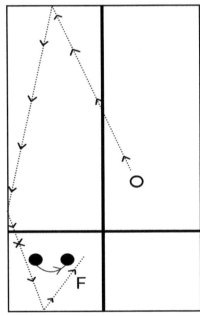

Fig. 21 Don't back up and take ball on backhand.

Fig. 22 Usually best to turn and take ball on forehand.

Learning to "come around" is another one of those frustrations you will not find easy to master at first. The ball, being so fast, will seem to run away from you.

Just remember two things:

1. hustle after the ball with short, speedy steps, keeping in mind that the angle is much greater than in Squash (see figs. 23 & 24) and
2. your racket must be back and cocked, ready to swing through when the ball arrives at the proper hitting position, which is preferably out in front of you.

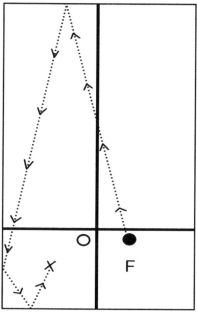

Fig. 23 Usual Squash Racquets angle and final bounce position.

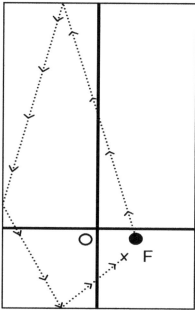

Fig. 24 Note wider, longer angle of Squash Tennis ball's final bounce position.

Finally, another aspect of the game of Squash that a beginner or a converted Squash player will find "unnatural" is the necessity of immediately moving forward when you see or sense your opponent going for a sharply hit up-and-down shot, either cross-court or "rail," that does not hit any of the side walls.

The Squash Rackets black ball is so much "deader" that the player usually has to go back first and then forward somewhat to be in the proper position to hit the ball as it rebounds off the back wall.

The tremendous speed of the Squash ball, however, does not require that you go toward the back wall first. To the contrary, you must charge forward instantly (even when your opponent's shot is heading toward the back wall) or else you will never be able to catch up to it as it comes rebounding off the back wall. Many a shot off the back wall is played from a position closer to the front wall than to the back.

Fundamental Strokes

The Squash stroke is more closely allied to the Squash rackets swing than to the Tennis swing. So read on for some great tips on the strokes of the game.

The Grip

Holding a squash racket can be very fiddly, and the correct grip is important.

Lay the handle across the top of your palm so it's placed just below the base of your fingers. The way you should grip a racket is a little like shaking hands with someone. Make sure your index finger protrudes upwards slightly away from the rest of the fingers. This makes a V-shape. You should hold onto the racket firmly but not rigidly.

If you are having trouble with accruacy of your shots check your grip.

Ground Strokes

The wrist and grip should be kept up and firm. The grip will be tighter at the moment of contact with the ball.

The forehand and backhand ground strokes need to be hit with a short, forearm stroke. There is no time and no reason to employ a long, high follow-through.

The head of the racket at the point of impact with the ball should be slightly "open". This slight side-spin cut, with the racket head tilting it back and hit a short shot, which will keep the ball low on the floor.

The spin will produce many "nicks," which are shots that hit a side wall and floor practically simultaneously and die. (See fig. 3 for position of racket at the moment of contact with ball.)

The follow-through is low and short. The racket head should go straight out and not wrapped around your body. The best way to "groove your strokes" and to keep the ball low is to consciously aim your racket head on your follow-through at the very, top of the "telltale."

As in all racket sports, the racket should do most of the work. Try to hit your shots crisply with the snap of your cocked wrist.

Whenever possible when playing ground strokes, you should turn sideways to the front wall.

Your weight should move toward the direction in which you are hitting at the moment of impact, and you should have your feet firm on the court floor. Because of the speed of the ball, you may not always have time to turn sideways.

Try always to be in the correct position of play before the ball gets there, thus allowing time for adjustment and proper stroking. Try to move to your position with short, quick steps.

It's a good idea to keep your weight on your toes, with your knees slightly bent. This will assist you to move in any direction during the rally.

Volleying or cutting off the ball before it hits the floor is similar to the tennis stroke.

The volley is a short "jab," with the racket head traveling forward no more than, try to aim in the direction of where you want the ball to go, and low.

The key purpose of the volley shot is to keep your opponent moving around, by cutting off the ball. Most players can run sideways with minimal effort, but will eventually get tired if you make them run the full length of the court.

Miscellaneous

You should try to keep your Squash strokes as low as possible. Playing the ball low gives you a better chance of getting "nicks" and keeps your opponent on the run.

When a ball is stuck to the side wall, don't attempt to "pick" it off the wall. It is far easier to try to "scrape" the ball off with a very loose wrist. Another way is to hit the ball right into the wall and hope it will angle off and travel to the front wall. (see figure 4)

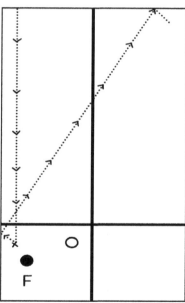

Fig. 3   Racquet open when contacting ball.

Fig. 4   To retrieve wall hugger, hit ball right into the wall.

Service

The best position before serving is to place your feet as close to the "T" area as possible. By doing this reduces the angle of the serve. Being in the "center" of the court is the best position to cover your opponent's return (see figure. 5).

The most effective service is attempt to hit as high as possible on the front wall to a "point" that will place the ball after bouncing as high which is also close to the side wall. Your opponent will have a harder time hitting the ball well because of its height and its closeness to the side wall.

If your service is struck with a slight cut, which will usually make the ball hug the wall. A semi-overhand, side-spin service is best employed from the right court, or a sliced underhand shot is used from the left side (see figure. 6).

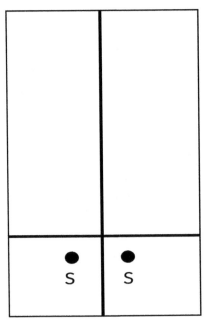

Fig. 5   Forehand and backhand service positions.

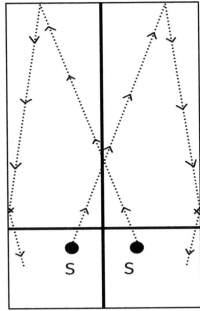

Fig. 6   Forehand and backhand lob services.

You should try to vary the service sometimes by hitting the ball harder right at your opponent. This could be either as a straight shot right down the middle of the court (figure. 7) or at a sharp angle that comes off the side wall and lands right at their feet (figure. 8).

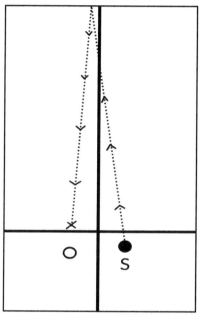

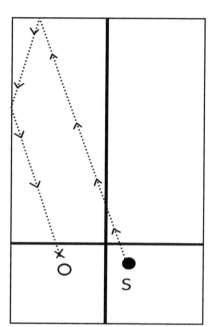

Fig. 7   Service straight down middle.

Fig. 8   In and out service angling into opponent.

The service is really the only stroke in Squash, which allows you the luxury of time before returning the ball.

Make sure you take full advantage by making sure you are settled and ready to receive the serve.

Chapter Six
Sports Nutrition for Squash Players

Featured Contributor - Kathy Roorda

Kathy has a strong passion for her profession. "The dietary and lifestyle choices we make in our lives can impact on our health status in either a good way or a bad way." Kathy wants to spread the word and educate people on the importance of nutrition in our health. "One bad decision can alter our health in a negative way. It's never too late, even one simple change can positively influence our health. Remember, the longer its left, the longer it will take to improve your health."

Kathy's passion for nutrition began after years of ill health. For many years she went to doctors and specialists with little improvement in her health. Finally she was fed up, and decided to take charge of her own health and do something about it. She decided to control her health rather than let her health control her. Kathy studied at Nature Care College for 6 years where she completed an Advanced Diploma of Nutritional Medicine and a Diploma of Nutrition. Her marks reflected her passion and determination for answers.

She continues to keep up to date with the industry and broaden her knowledge and education.

Upon completion of her studies, Kathy now has the knowledge to maintain her health and reduce symptoms during flare ups. She is now able to lead a better quality of life with reduced problems.

It is this experience that has led Kathy to help others achieve optimal health. "I know that if I had more knowledge when I was younger regarding health and nutrition, I may not have experienced the many problems I have had to face over the years."

"I believe that any positive change is a good change, and looking after our inner body will help improve our health dramatically. It's like putting fuel in a car, if you put the wrong fuel in, it won't go and the engine will be damaged.

Our body works much the same, you put the wrong foods in, over a period of time, the organs that keep the body going will eventually become damaged or deteriorate, and their functions will be reduced, and thus lead to poor health."

Kathy's personal experience and education has led her to an interest in health issues relating to the digestive system. "Gut related problems may include: pain, inflammation, IBS, constipation, diarrhea, nausea, flatulence, swelling, joint pain, allergies, sensitivities, hay fever, food & environmental intolerances, stress, anxiety, fatigue, skin problems, and feeling unwell.

It's amazing how many of these symptoms relate to our gut health. A good functioning gut and liver reduces risks of health problems and minimizes long term or chronic health issues." Kathy's GIT program will help you get back on track and put the bounce back in you – revitalised and refreshed!

Kathy also has an interest in sports nutrition, and her research in this area so far has given her the acquired knowledge for sports nutrition. If you're looking at starting an exercise program, Hills Nutrition 4 Health can get you started on the right track with optimal nutrition and recovery plans.

An initial consultation, up to 1 ½ hours includes a full systems review, nutritional information sheets, and individualised treatment plans. Kathy is an accredited member of the Australian Traditional Medicine Society, and health fund rebates are available with participating funds.

Her service also offers home visits as required, and discounts for pensioners and children under 12 years of age.

Contact Kathy

 (02) 9890 9213

www.hillsnutrition4health.com.au

Naturopathic Nutrition

General Naturopathic Nutrition Guidelines

Nutritional Medicine is based on a diet that promotes health by eating whole, natural foods. Nutritional supplements may also be used as complementary agents. A Naturopathic Practitioner looks at the whole person and treats each person individually. Education is a key factor to a healthy mind, body and soul.

The principles of Naturopathic Medicine include:

- The Healing Power of Nature: Vis Medicatrix Naturae
- First Do Not Harm: Primun Non Nocere
- Find The Cause: Tolle Causam
- Doctor as Teacher: Docere
- Treat The Whole Person
- Preventive Medicine

Eating for Optimal Health

1. Eat a Mix of Fruits and Vegetables that includes all colours

This includes a range of colourful foods – red, orange, yellow, green, blue, and purple.

This provides the body with phytochemicals (pigments) such as carotenes, chlorophyll and flavonoids; dietary fibre; enzymes; antioxidants; and nutrients necessary for body function and protection against diseases.

Anticancer Phytochemicals

Carotenes, Courmarin, Dithiolthiones, Flavonoids, Isoflavonoids, Lignans, Limonoids, Polyphenols, Sterols.

Actions of Phytochemicals

Antioxidants, enhance immune function, anti-tumor properties, modulate hormone receptors, enhance detoxification, and block carcinogens, block oestrogen receptors, and block cancer causing compounds from damaging cells.

Examples: Dark vegetables – carrots, squash, spinach, kale, tomatoes, celery, greens, sweet potatoes;

Fruits – cantaloupe, apricots, citrus fruits, berries, cherries; flax seeds/oil, whole grains, nuts, seeds, soy, broccoli, cabbage, brussel sprouts, fennels, beets, etc...

Coloured Mix of Fruits and Vegetables

Red - apples, bell peppers, cherries, cranberries, grapefruit, grapes, plums, radishes, raspberries, strawberries, watermelon, tomatoes.

(Contain lycopene – may help fight prostate cancer and heart disease)

Dark Green – artichoke, asparagus, bell peppers, broccoli, brussel sprouts, cucumber, grapes, beans, honeydew melons, kale, leeks, lettuce, peas, spinach, turnip greens, chard.

(Contain Lutein and Zeaxanthin – may help protect against age-related eye disease)

Yellow and Light Green – apples, avocado, bell peppers, bok choy, banana, cabbage, cauliflower, celery, fennel, kiwifruit, lemons, lettuce, limes, onions, pears, pineapple, squash, yellow zucchini.

Orange – apricots, bell peppers, butternut squash, cantaloupe, carrots, mangoes, oranges, papaya, pumpkin, sweet potatoes.

Purple – beets, blackberries, blueberries, cabbage, cherries, currants, eggplants, grapes, onions, red pears, plums, radishes.

(Contain anthocyanins – may help protect body from cancer)

2. Reduce Exposure to Pesticides

- Eat less animal fat, meat, eggs, cheese, milk (tendency to concentrate pesticides)
- Buy organic
- Get to know your local grocery store manager
- Buy local produce in season
- Remove pesticide residues by soaking produce in mild additive-free soap such as ivory or pure castile soap, or a natural biodegradable cleanser – health food stores. (Spray on food, gently scrub, and rinse.)

3. Eat to Support Blood Sugar Control

Eat a low GI and low GL diet. (Low GI - <55) GI refers to how quickly blood sugar levels rise after the food is eaten. GL considers the GI and how much carbohydrate is contained in a food serving. (Low GL - < 11) If a GI is high and the GL is low in a particular food, blood sugar levels will not rise greatly as long as portions of the food are reasonable. Eg: Watermelon – GI = 72, GL = 4 (120g).

Reduce consumption of refined sugars, and white flour products. High sugar leads to poor blood sugar regulation, obesity, Type 2 DM, heart disease, and cancer.

4. Reduce Intake of Meat and Other Animal Foods

Meat contains saturated fat, carcinogenic compounds – pesticide residues, heterocyclic amines, and polycyclic aromatic hydrocarbons. When the meat is well cooked, it contains higher amine levels. Some research suggests high intake of animal products may increase cancers

– colon, breast, prostate, lung, and heart disease.
Cured and smoked meats that contain nitrates / nitrites (preservative) may increase the risk of cancer. In the stomach, these chemicals in the food react with amino acids, and form nitrosamines (highly carcinogenic).

Eg: ham, hot dogs, bacon, jerky.

5. Eat the Right Type of Fats

Decrease saturated fat and trans fat intake and increase omega-3 fatty acids and monounsaturated fatty acids. Cells do not function well unless cell membranes contain the right type of fats. Good sources include: oily fish – sardines, salmon, tuna (avoid shark, swordfish, king mackerel – high mercury content), olive oil, nuts and seeds – flax seeds/oil, linseeds/oil.

6. Low Salt Intake

Balance potassium, sodium, chloride, and magnesium intake. Too much salt in diet can disrupt electrolyte balance. Tips: Reduce flavouring foods with salt and use herbs, spices, and lemon juice as alternative; read food labels carefully – sodium content, reduce consumption of canned vegetables or soups (high in sodium).

Optimal Potassium / Sodium ratio – greater than 5 : 1. Fresh fruit and vegetable intake provides higher potassium to sodium ratio.

7. Avoid Food Additives

Food additives are used to preserve foods and enhance flavour. They include: preservatives, artificial colours, flavours, and acidifiers. Food additives may cause allergies, sensitivities in individuals. The elimination of additives may reduce allergic conditions such as asthma, eczema, and hives; and sensitivities.

8. Reduce Foodborne Illness

Tips: Cook meat, poultry, and eggs thoroughly; check internal meat with a thermometer (eg: ground beef temp should be 160F, poultry – 185F, and egg yolk should be firm); wash hands, utensil, and cutting boards, and use separate boards for meats and fruit / vegetables, cooked meats should be separate from raw meats; fresh fruit and vegetables should be washed before use, and greens soaked (mild soap can be used).

9. Drink Plenty of Water Each Day

Drink at least 8-12 glasses of water each day (adults), 4-5 glasses (children). Water is necessary for the body to function correctly. Water is necessary to transport chemicals and nutrients to cells and tissues, component of blood, component of all cells, elimination of wastes, and maintain body temperature.

Healthy Food Guideline (each day)

Eat Most:

- Fresh Vegetables (combination of raw and cooked, and a variety of colours). Approx 5 to 7 serves.
- Whole grains – cereals-oats, polenta; bread – rye, barley; pastas; brown riceor low GI (basmati). Approx 3 to 5 serves
- Fruit. Approx 2 to 3 serves.
- Unsalted Nuts and Legumes – beans, lentils, peas. Approx 1 to 3 serves.
- Nuts, Seeds, Sprouts, Vegetable Oils – flax, olive (raw). Cook with cold pressed olive, macadamia and sesame oil.

Eat Moderate:

- Fish, Seafood.
- Lean Meat, Chicken, (no skin) Eggs.

Eat Least:

- Dairy – yoghurt, milk, cheese (limit intake due to saturated fat content). Approx 1 to 2 serves.
- Calcium enriched soymilk or calcium supplement.
- Wine in moderation, preferably red wine (antioxidant properties)

Include:

- 8 – 12 glasses pure water each day.
- Herbal Teas, Freshly squeezed vegetable and fruit juices.
- Regular Daily Exercise (aerobic, strength, stretching), Relaxation time.

Avoid:

- Refined Carbohydrates / Sugars.
- Saturated / Trans Fats - hydrogenated oils, margarine, butter, deep fried foods, fast foods.
- Processed / Packaged Foods – white rice, white bread, sweets.
- Cured / processed meats – hams, hot dogs, bacon, jerky.
- Limit Salt intake.
- Stress.

Vegetables, fruits, nuts, seeds, whole grains, and legumes are packed with nutrients – Carbohydrates, Protein, Vitamins and Dietary Fibre.

Fish, seafood, lean meat, chicken, eggs, milk, cheese, and yoghurt are packed with Protein, Minerals (esp. iron and calcium), and B group vitamins.

Fibre

Fibre is a carbohydrate, made up of different types of sugars. These consist of: Simple sugars – glucose, fructose, sucrose, maltose, and lactose (1-2 sugar molecules); Oligosaccharides (3-10 glucose molecules); Starch Polysaccharides (more than 10 glucose molecules joined together); Non-Starch Polysaccharides – xylose, arabinose, mannose (more than 10 sugar molecules).

Dietary Fibre is required to keep the digestive system healthy, and it stabilizes glucose and cholesterol levels.

Australian Heart Foundation recommends adults consume 30g of fibre daily and children 10g plus an extra gram for every year of age.

Soluble Fibre involved in: lowering blood cholesterol, and reducing constipation. It slows down the rate of digestion. It forms a gel due to its water containing capacity. Soluble Fibre includes: pectins, gums, and mucilage (mainly in plant cells). Good sources include: fruits, vegetables, oatbran, barley, seed husks, flaxseed, psyllium, dried beans, lentils, peas, soy milk, soybeans, baked beans.

Insoluble Fibre involved in: preventing constipation and associated haemorrhoids by adding bulk to faeces; speeds up the time that food passes through the gut ('roughage'); resistant to digestion and fermented by bacteria to produce fatty acids for a healthy gut wall. Insoluble fibre includes: cellulose, hemicellulose, and lignin (structural part of plant cell walls) – Fruit & Veggies: Carrots, broccoli, peas; brown rice, wheat bran, whole wheat products.

Resistant Starch – Fermented in the gut, resulting in beneficial effects on the bowel, and blood cholesterol levels. Found in whole grains, potatoes, lentils, firm bananas, 'Hi-Maize' – added to bread and breakfast cereals.

An increase in fibre is important for older people, as the digestive system slows down as we age; fibrous foods are often bulky and filling, and low in fat; a person feels full for longer, and fibre delays absorption of sugars from the intestines into the blood to help maintain blood sugar levels. Therefore, high fibre may assist in obesity and diabetes mellitus.

A low fibre diet may contribute to: constipation, hemorrhoids, diverticulitis, irritable bowel syndrome, obesity, coronary heart disease, diabetes mellitus, colon cancer.

How to Increase Fibre Intake

- Breakfast Cereals – containing barley, wheat, oats
- Wholemeal or Multigrain bread and brown rice

- Increase Vegetable intake
- Snacks – fruit, dried fruit, nuts or wholemeal crackers

Suggestions

Food	Fibre Content (grams)
2 whole wheat cereal biscuits – weet-bix or vita brits	3.2g
4 slices wholegrain bread	5.7g
1 cup baked beans	7.0g
1 cup cannellini beans (canned)	16.0g
Fruit –apple / pear / passionfruit	3.5g / 4.0g / 5.0g
1 cup frozen mixed vegetables	8.6g
1 cup wholemeal spaghetti	6.0g
1 small boiled potato with skin (100g)	2.8g
20 almonds	3.5g
2 wholemeal dry biscuits	1.5g

Tips

- Eat Wholefoods (unprocessed / unrefined) – fresh raw fruits and vegetables, nuts, seeds, sprouts, unpolished grains, unprocessed meat, poultry, fish
- Drink plenty of water each day (8-12 glasses)
- Ensure adequate fibre intake (soluble and insoluble) – fruits and vegetables, grains, legumes
- Chew foods well to assist digestion and eat slowly
- Eat smaller regular meals, do not over eat
- Buy fresh foods regularly, eat foods in season
- Eat a balance of raw and cooked vegetables (help protect against type 2 diabetes mellitus, stroke, cardiovascular disease, cancer, high blood pressure)
- Eat a variety of colours, and try something new each week
- Eat mostly healthy foods and occasionally treat yourself (challenges your body and satisfies your mind and soul), develop good eating habits
- Get to know your local produce managers (pesticides and additive free foods)

- Develop positive attitude towards healthy eating

- Eat a balanced diet, choose a variety of foods, and rotate foods regularly (ensures optimal nutrient intake, and avoids food resistance)
- Ensure daily exercise, minimize stress levels (yoga, deep breathing, massage etc)

Resources

- Heart Foundation
- Nutrition Australia – www.nutritionaustralia.org
- NHMRC – www.nhmrc.gov.au
- Diabetes Association

7 Day Sample Nutritional Menu Plan

MONDAY

Breakfast

- ¾ cup oatmeal topped with banana & blueberries
- 1 glass soy, almond / coconut or low-fat milk
- 1 slice whole grain bread with avocado

Morning Tea

- 1 piece fruit (apple, pear, pineapple)
- 30-50gm nuts (almonds/walnuts)

Lunch

- 1 medium pita bread topped with 2 tsp homemade hummus, ½ cup spinach, 2 slices tomato, 3-4 slices roast lamb or chicken
- 1 serve veggie sticks (celery, carrot, cucumber)

Snack

- Nuts & Seeds mix (1/4 cup almonds, sunflower seeds, raisins or sultanas, ½ oz pumpkin seeds)

Dinner

- Casserole (2/3 cup brown rice, ½ cup mixed beans, 1 tsp safflower or olive oil, 1 cup broccoli, ½ cup yellow squash, ¼ cup onion)
- ¾ cup cooked Kale

Dessert

- 1 tub low fat yoghurt topped with seasonal fruit (Plain Greek yoghurt with beneficial bacteria and additive free recommended)

TUESDAY

Breakfast

- Homemade toasted muesli or 2 Vita Brits
- 1 slice toast (whole grain) with almond spread + honey
- 1 glass soy, almond or reduced fat milk.
- 1 glass freshly squeezed pineapple juice

Morning Tea

- Fruit salad with groundnut seed mix.

Lunch

- 1 wholegrain sandwich with watercress, grated carrot, chicken or tuna, avocado
- - 2 kiwi fruits or 1 pear

Snack

- Banana & Blueberry Smoothie

Dinner

- 1 piece fish (Salmon, Cod, Herring, Mackeral) with lemon & parsley
- 2 cups steamed veggies

Dessert

- Baked apple with plain yoghurt

WEDNESDAY

Breakfast

- 1 cup gluten free porridge (millet, quinoa, buckwheat, dates)
- 1 cup soy, almond or low-fat milk.
- 1 cup fresh pineapple pieces
- 1 slice wholegrain toast with mashed strawberries

Morning Tea

- 2 Homemade nutty muesli squares
- 1 banana

Lunch

- Tuna salad (Sml tin tuna in olive oil, lettuce, tomato, cucumber, grated carrot, celery, baby spinach, lemon juice)
- 1-2 slices whole grain bread with avocado

Snack

- Toasted corn wrap or mountain bread with egg, salad & avocado

Dinner

- Chicken Tacos with lettuce, tomato, avocado, olives, cucumber, low-fat cheese, grated carrot, walnuts

Dessert

- Fruit Salad & 1 tbs frozen yoghurt, 1 tbs LSA (ground linseeds, sunflower seeds, almonds).

THURSDAY

Breakfast

- Bircher Muesli
- 1 piece toast with almond spread
- 1 glass fresh apple, ginger & carrot juice

OR

- Banana & Berry Smoothie
- Morning Tea
- Veggie sticks with hummus dip
- Fruit

Lunch

- Chicken Cranberry Rissoles with leafy green salad & hummus dipping sauce

Snack

- Vietnamese rolls: Rice paper rolls filled with chicken, carrot, lettuce, bean sprouts, mint leaves, fresh chives
- Sweet chili dipping sauce

Dinner

- Baked frittata
- Leafy green salad with walnuts, slithered apples, radish, lemon juice, flaxseed or olive oil

Dessert

- Frozen fruit iceblocks & yoghurt

FRIDAY

Breakfast

- Fruit salad (pawpaw, pineapple, orange, apple, pear, kiwi, strawberries, grapes)
- S.L.A.P 1 tbs ground sunflower seeds, flaxseeds, almonds, pepitas; add little grape juice & coconut oil, stir, add to fruit salad

Morning Tea

Banana & Berry Smoothie

Lunch

- Homemade pumpkin soup
- Serve with croutons just before eating
- 1 piece fruit

Afternoon Tea

- Rice paper roll

Dinner

- Homemade pizzas with favourite toppings on pita bread

OR

- Chicken, prawn & vegetable stir-fry

Dessert

- Wholemeal spelt pancakes

SATURDAY

Breakfast

- Scrambled eggs on toast with baby spinach, cooked baby tomatoes, onion, mushrooms, and zucchini

Morning Tea

- Mango & Banana Smoothie with ¼ cup Carmen's muesli added just before consumption for that extra crunch

Lunch

- Chicken strips coated with equal parts of parmesan and polenta, baked in oven until cooked through. Serve with lemon wedges
- Bowl of salad with favourite veggies & Balsamic dressing

Afternoon Tea

- 2 Nutty Muesli squares

or

- Carmen's Fruit Muesli bar

Dinner

- Homemade spaghetti bolognese or lasagna
- If eating out, try to choose healthier options such as:

BBQ chicken & greek salad; grilled fish & salad; Stirfry with steamed rice; Lean meat & veggies; vegetarian pizza, sushi, etc.

Dessert

- Fruit Salad
- If eating out: fruit salad with yoghurt or sorbet; banana cake, carrot cake, frozen yoghurt etc.

SUNDAY

Breakfast

- French toast with berries, yoghurt & nuts & seeds. (walnuts, almonds, pecans, pepitas)

Morning Tea

- Fruit Salad Smoothie

Lunch

- Homemade Sushi

Afternoon Tea

- 2 Nutty muesli squares
- 1 piece fruit

Dinner

- Roast Lamb & Veggies

Dessert

- Blueberry Frozen Yoghurt

Drinks / Fluids

- Water (2 litres daily) Increase with physical activity
- Freshly squeezed fruit & veggie juice daily
- Diluted fruit juice with 50/50 juice and water
- Green Tea, chamomile tea, ginger tea.

Snack options

- Fresh Fruit
- Unsulphured Dried Fruit
- Veggie Sticks (carrot, celery, cucumber, capsicum) with hummus dip or nut dip
- Nuts and Seeds (almonds, walnuts, pecans, pepitas, sunflower seeds, etc)
- Rice cakes with avocado, honey, nut spread, banana, ricotta, etc.
- Frozen banana iceblocks
- Frozen blended fruit iceblocks
- Plain popcorn
- Smoothie
- Toast with nut spread
- Egg & cucumber sandwich
- Toasted sandwiches (baked beans, or egg, or cheese & tomato, or chicken & avocado, etc)
- Salad wrap (mountain bread or corn diego wraps or pita bread)
- Vietnamese rolls (Rice paper rolls)
- Sushi rolls
- Homemade muffins
- Mini quiches
- Hard boiled eggs
- Corn crackers with hummus
- Fresh fruit with yoghurt
- Homemade chips – Thinly sliced baked sweet potato drizzled with herbs & olive oil
- Homemade pancakes with cooked apple
- Homemade biscuits or muesli bars
- - Rice crackers
- Mini pizzas on flat bread (corn diego wraps or pita bread)

Tips & Recommendations

- Eat within 20-30 mins post exercise, with a carb / protein ratio of 4 to 1. This will allow replacement of glycogen stores ready for next workout. It will also help blunt cortisol, & improve the immune system. Insulin is most active after exercise, and after 2 hrs, reduces to half potency.
- Eat medium to high GI foods post exercise to quickly replace glycogen stores.
- Pre-workout, eat low GI foods to sustain energy.
- Eat regularly after exercise to ensure maximum glycogen replenishment.
- Ensure adequate fluid intake daily, especially during and after exercise.
- During flare-ups of the GIT, go back to basics and consider eating low reactive foods such as lamb, rice, pears, or foods you don't normally react to. EFA's, fish, cabbage, garlic, onion, ginger may assist gastrointestinal healing and reduce inflammation.
- Adequate daily sunlight is important, approximately 20 mins / day to achieve adequate vitamin D levels. Vit D is important for the absorption of calcium, bone health, and immune modulation.
- Increase Antioxidants - may help reduce inflammation.

Exercise Recommendations

- Aim for 3-4 days minimum of physical activity, at least 30-40 mins daily.
- Exercise Suggestions: Squash, swimming, tennis, walking, aerobics, volleyball, netball, bicycling, dancing, zumba, skipping, treadmill, yoga, pilates; Resistance exercise - light hand weights, etc.
- To achieve all areas of physical fitness, vary activities including cardio-respiratory fitness, muscle strength, flexibility, mobility, and coordination.
- Ensure drink enough fluids before, during, and after exercise. Cold water is the best fluid. Sports drinks containing 4% - 8% carbohydrates and diluted fruit juice is also okay.
- Other ideas that increase physical activities without dramatic lifestyle changes: Use public transport rather than taking the car. This usually involves at least some walking to and from bus stops; use stairs instead of lifts; walk or ride a bike to and from work, and friend's house; family domestic duties;

- Organise family activity days such as bike riding, volleyball, soccer, tennis, swimming, etc. This gives valuable family time together as well as encouraging physical activity in children, and setting up for a lifetime of being physically active, into adulthood, and thus reducing the risk of obesity and health problems later in life.

Recipes

BREAKFAST

Pear and Flaxseed Smoothie

In a blender add the following ingredients:

- 1 cup soy or almond / coconut milk
- 1tbs flaxseeds
- 2 pears, peeled, cored
- Dash of honey

Banana & Blueberry Smoothie

- 1 banana
- ¼ cup blueberries
- 2 handfuls almonds or 1 handful each of walnuts and almonds
- 6 ice cubes
- 2 tbsp natural yoghurt
- 1 glass low fat milk, almond, coconut or soy milk
- 1 tbsp honey
- ¼ cup water

Combine all ingredients in a blender. Makes about 2-3 large glasses. Use other combinations of fruit such as banana & mango; mixed berries, etc.

2 Pieces of Whole Grain Toast (Soy & Linseed)

Top with avocado, thinly sliced apple, red onion, chopped walnuts.
Tuna, Tomato, Basil, Linseed and Soy Yoghurt Bruschetta

- 2 Pieces, toasted wholegrain, Sourdough Bread or gluten free bread, sprayed with little olive oil
- 1 small tin tuna in water or olive oil
- 1-2 cloves garlic, crushed or finely chopped
- 1-2 chopped tomatoes
- Freshly ground black pepper
- 2 tbsp torn basil
- 1 tsp linseeds or flaxseeds
- 1 tbsp low fat, soy yoghurt

Method

Toast bread on a hot plate or in a pan. Add tuna, tomato and garlic to each toasted piece of bread. Add pepper, torn basil, and seeds. Dollop each piece with soy yoghurt. Serve.

Bircher Muesli

- 150g rolled oats
- 225 ml apple juice
- 1 grated apple
- 125 ml yoghurt
- 150g blueberries
- 2 nectarines or peaches sliced
- 2 tbsp honey

Method

Combine oats and apple juice in a mixing bowl, cover and refrigerate overnight.

Stir the apple and yoghurt into the soaked oats, and divide between 4 serving bowls. Top with blueberries and peaches, and drizzle with honey.

Fruit salad with Ground Nut/Seed Mix

- pineapple
- orange
- apple
- pear
- kiwi
- strawberries, blueberries
- passionfruit
- grapes
- S.L.A.P - 1 tbs ground sunflower seeds, flaxseeds, almonds, pepitas; add little grape juice & coconut oil, stir, add to fruit salad.

LUNCH / DINNER

Salmon and Dukkah Salad with Avocado Dressing

- Canned salmon added to salad at the time of consumption. Alternative: Cook fresh salmon the night before, coated with dukkah mix, and add to salad mix when cooled; or add dukkah mix to the canned salmon salad. Keep freshly cooked salmon cool until ready to eat.
- 2 tsp pitted black olives
- ½ red onion
- ½ sliced avocado
- 1 shredded carrot
- 1 thinly sliced apple
- Handful of spinach
- 1-2 tbsp of dukkah mix (sesame seeds, almonds, hazelnuts, cumin, coriander, sea salt, pepper)

Avocado Dressing

In a blender combine the following ingredients until smooth:

- 1 avocado
- ½ lemon
- ½ cup water
- ½ tsp dill
- ¼ tsp sea salt

Samosa with Minted Yoghurt

- 1 clove garlic, finely chopped
- 1 carrot, diced
- 1 onion, chopped
- ½ cup peas
- 1/2 sweet potato, chopped
- 1 celery, chopped
- ½ cup coriander, chopped
- 1 tsp curry powder
- 1 cup chicken stock
- Lemon juice
- 2 beaten eggs
- 4 corn tortillas

1. Preheat oven to 180°C. In pan over medium heat, add garlic, onion, carrot, potato, celery, peas. Stir. Add chicken stock, lemon juice, and stir. Cook with lid on for 20 mins. Set aside.

2. Dip corn tortillas in egg, then place in a sandwich press for a few seconds, and keep warm in a tea towel.

3. Put 2 tbsp of the filling into each tortilla and fold over into a triangle. Cook in oven until golden brown. Serve with minted yoghurt and mixed green salad. Makes 4.

Minted Yoghurt

- ½ cup plain yoghurt
- 2 tbsp mint, finely chopped
- 2 tbsp coriander finely chopped
- 1 cucumber, diced
- Lemon juice
- Salt & pepper

1. Mix together all ingredients except for lemon juice. Add lemon juice and salt& pepper. Cover and put in fridge for ½ - 1 hr to set. Serve over Samosa.

Sushi

- 1 cup basmati rice
- 12 sheets nori, cut in half crossways
- Tuna or chicken or prawns
- 1 cucumber cut into thin matchsticks
- 2 carrots cut into thin matchsticks
- 1 avocado cut into strips
- 100g alfalfa sprouts

Method

1. Bring rice to boil over a high heat, then reduce heat to low and cook until rice is just tender.

2. Put nori sheets on two plates and divide the protein – chicken or tuna or prawn; cucumber, carrots, and avocado onto 2 additional plates. Divide sprouts into 2 small bowls. Divide rice into 2 serving bowls.

3. To assemble, put 1 piece of nori, shiny side down with 2 tbsp rice. Top with protein, 1-3 strips of veggies and some sprouts, then roll the sushi upwards to form a log. Dip in sweet chili sauce to serve.

Chicken & Rice Paper Rolls

- 1-2 cooked chicken breast fillets (depending on size), or prawns
- 12 rice paper rounds
- 1 head butter lettuce
- 1 capsicum, seeded and cut into strips
- 1 carrot, peeled and cut into strips
- 75g bean sprouts
- 24 mint leaves
- Sweet chili sauce, to serve

Method

Cut chicken into strips. Dip one rice paper round briefly into a bowl of warm water and drain. Spread on a work bench and top rice paper with a small lettuce leaf, capsicum and carrot strip, a few bean sprouts, a couple of mint leaves and strip of chicken. Fold base up and then fold sides in and roll up firmly. Serve with sweet chilli sauce. If short of time try BBQ chicken.

Chicken Cranberry Rissoles

Served with Fennel Salad or Mash & Steamed Veggies

Serves 4

Ingredients

- 500gm Chicken Mince
- 1/2 chopped onion
- 1 chopped Zucchini
- 1 grated carrot
- 1 cup Finely chopped baby spinach & Rocket
- Turmeric
- Mixed Herbs
- Fennel Seeds
- 1/4 cup dried cranberries
- 2 tbs pepitas
- 2 handfuls gluten free breadcrumbs
- 1 egg

Method

Combine all ingredients and roll into little balls and place in hot pan with olive oil. Flatten each rissole and cook on each side until golden brown.

Serve with Mash and Veggies or fresh baby spinach, thinly sliced apple and orange segments, and fennel salad topped with balsamic dressing.

Optional: Serve Rissoles with hummus.

SNACKS / DESSERT

Nutty Muesli Squares

- 115g unsalted butter
- 4 tbsp honey
- 25g unrefined caster sugar
- 250g porridge oats
- 25g dried cranberries, blueberries or apricots
- 25g chopped, stoned dates or raisins
- 25g chopped pecans or walnuts
- 70g flaked almonds

Method:

1. Preheat oven to 190°C. Grease a 20cm square baking tin with olive oil.

2. Melt the butter with the honey and sugar in a saucepan and stir together. Add the remaining ingredients and mix thoroughly.

3. Place the mixture into the tin and press down well. Bake for 20-30 mins.

4. Remove from oven and leave to cool in the tin. Cut into squares.

Wholemeal Spelt Pancakes

- 325g wholemeal spelt flour
- 1 tbsp baking powder
- ½ tsp salt
- 1 beaten egg
- 350ml lite or soy milk
- 2 tbsp olive oil, plus extra for frying
- ½ cup blueberries, chopped strawberries or chopped banana
- Honey and lemon wedges to serve

Method:

1. In a small bowl mix together the flour, baking powder, and salt. In a medium bowl, whisk together the egg, milk and olive oil. Pour the dry mixture into the wet ingredients and whisk until smooth. Fold in the blueberries with a wooden spoon.

2. Heat a little olive oil in a pan and drop 1-2 tbsp of the batter into the pan. If the batter is too thick, add a little more milk. Cook for 2 mins or until bubbles appear on the surface, and the underside is brown. Flip over and brown the other side.

3. Transfer the cooked pancakes to a plate and keep warm, while you make the remaining pancakes.

4. Spread each pancake with a little margarine, drizzle with honey, and a squeeze of lemon.

SAUCES

Pesto

Blend the following ingredients, in a blender for 2-3 mins, to a paste.

- 2 tsp extra virgin olive oil
- 1 clove garlic, peeled and chopped
- 2 tbsp pine nuts
- 1 cup basil leaves
- 3 tbsp grated parmesan cheese

Hummus

- 2 cups chickpeas, soaked, rinsed and cooked for 1 hour.
- Juice of 1/2 lemon
- 3 fresh basil leaves
- Fresh parsley / Chives
- 2 tbsp tahini
- 1 tsp salt
- 1 cup water

Place all ingredients in a blender. Blend. Add extra water if needed to make a smooth paste.

Optional: Add 1-2 cloves roasted garlic.

Nutrient Sources

- **P**rotein Sources – (Portion size: Same size and thickness of palm of hand). Poultry, lean meat, fish, eggs, legumes, nuts, dairy if not allergic / intolerant. Animal sources – primary proteins contain all the amino acids (complete); Plant sources - secondary proteins (incomplete). The combination of two of the following will give you a complete protein – nuts, grains/seeds, legumes/pulses. (eg. Combine grains and legumes within one meal or one day).

- **Non-Dairy Protein** – Tofu, grilled fish, tuna, beans + grains, ground nuts + seeds.

- **Low-risk carbohydrates** - (Portion size: 2 palm sized portions). Asparagus, cabbage family, capsicum, chickpeas, eggplant, lentils, lettuce, mushrooms, onions, apples, apricots, cherries, grapes, melons, oranges, peaches, pears, strawberries.

- **Moderate risk carbohydrates** - (Portion size: 1 palm sized portion). Baked beans, carrots, corn, peas, potato, sweet potato, banana, dates, figs, fruit juices, bread, pasta, rice, tacos / tortillas, relishes.

You can choose to combine 1 ½ palms low-risk carbs and ½ palm moderate risk carbs in the same meal. (Carb portions should total 2 palm sizes, but no more than 1 palm size portion of moderate risk carbs).

- **Healthy Fats and Oils** – Nuts (almonds, hazelnuts, walnuts); Seeds (flaxseed, pumpkin, sesame); Cooking oils (olive, sesame); avocado, mayonnaise (eggless or soya); Dressings (olive, flaxseed, pumpkin, walnut oil); Fresh herbs or lemon juice can be added for flavour; fish.

- **Folic acid sources** – Green leafy vegetables, eggs, enriched bread & cereals, lentils, legumes, asparagus, lettuce, spinach, fresh wheat germ, broccoli, raw unsalted nuts, fresh orange juice, oranges, strawberries, chicken liver, beef liver, dried peas & beans.

- **B1 (Thiamine) Vitamin sources** – Rice bran, wheat germ, oat bran, whole grains, pork, fortified cereals, sunflower seeds, pine nuts, sesame seeds, pistachio nuts, buckwheat, lima beans, pinto beans, mung beans, peas, egg yolks, Brazil nuts, broad beans.

- **B2 (Riboflavin) Vitamin sources** – Fortified cereals, poultry, wheat germ, almonds, mushrooms, millet, soybeans, parsley, cashew nuts, rice bran, lentils, sesame & sunflower seeds, rye, broccoli, mung beans, avocado, asparagus, dark leafy greens.

- **B3 (Niacin) Vitamin sources** – Fish, salmon, tuna, poultry, red meat, pork, fortified cereals, wheat germ, legumes, mushrooms, brown rice, sesame & sunflower seeds, buckwheat, peaches, bulghur wheat, wholemeal pasta.

- **B5 (Pantothenate) Vitamin sources** – Organ meat, avocado, hazelnuts, mushroom, sunflower seeds, eggs, soybeans, broccoli, wheat germ, wheat bran, wholegrain bread and cereals, green leafy veggies, beans and peas.

- **B6 (Pyridoxine) Vitamin sources** – Whole grains, muesli, fortified cereals, chicken, tuna, salmon, cod, sunflower seeds, lentils, kidney beans, avocado, peas, nuts, banana, walnuts, lima beans, buckwheat, navy beans, brown rice, hazelnuts, garbanzo beans, pinto beans, kale, spinach, turnip greens, sweet red peppers, sweet potato, sardines, brussel sprouts, cauliflower, red cabbage, leek.

- **B12 (Cobalamin) Vitamin sources** – Poultry, fish, beef, fortified cereals, eggs, dairy, sardines, salmon, herring, low fat cottage cheese.

- **Iron sources** – Red meat, poultry, apricots, parsley, pine nuts, soybeans, baked beans, sunflower & pumpkin seeds, wheat germ, enriched cereals, green leafy veggies, prune juice, eggs, millet, parsley, kidney beans, almonds, hazelnuts, whole grains, sardines, Jerusalem artichokes, beet greens, walnuts, spinach, lentils, pecans, sesame seeds.

- **Zinc sources** – Fish, herring, sardines, tuna, red meat, lamb, turkey, chicken, sesame seeds, sunflower seeds, pepitas, walnuts, almonds, cashews, muesli, wheat germ, tomato sauce, egg yolks, ginger, whole grains, pecans, lima beans, buckwheat, green peas, hazelnuts, turnips, paprika, thyme, cinnamon, black pepper.

- **Dairy Calcium Sources** – Yoghurt, milk, cheese.

- **Dairy free Calcium sources** – Seaweed, collard leaves, beet, dandelion and turnip greens, parsley, watercress, broccoli, spinach, sesame seeds (hulled), tahini paste, almonds, brazil nuts, tofu, olives, soybeans, salmon & sardines (with bones).

- **Essential Fatty Acid sources** – Salmon, cod, mackerel, herring, soybeans, flaxseeds, sunflower seeds, sesame seeds, flaxseed oil, soybean oil, sunflower oil, sesame oil, walnuts.

- **Vitamin A sources** – Apricots, carrots, cod oil, salmon oil, green leafy veggies, mint, egg yolk, poultry, cornmeal, parsley, sweet potato, raw spinach, mango, butternut squash, beet greens, chives, watercress, winter squash, tomato, cantaloupe, broccoli.

- **Vit C sources** – Blackcurrants, broccoli, citrus fruit, parsley, peppers, pineapple, potato, raw cabbage, strawberries, brussel sprouts, papaya, kiwi fruit, mango, lychees, oranges, sprouts, kale, collards, turnip greens, cauliflower, lemons, watercress, asparagus, cantaloupe, green onions, tangerines, lima beans, green peas, radishes, raspberries, honeydew melon, tomato.

- **Vit E sources** – Almonds, whole grains, wheat germ, raw unsalted nuts, raw unsalted seeds, sprouts, green leafy veggies, eggs, soybean oil, wheat germ oil, walnuts, cashews, sunflower seeds, safflower seeds, avocado, brown rice.

- **Magnesium sources** – Millet, whole grains, green leafy veggies, muesli, almonds, cashews, legumes, buckwheat, pecans, walnuts, beet greens, spinach, brown rice, corn, avocado, parsley, dry beans, garlic, fresh green peas, banana, sweet potato, blackberries, beets, broccoli, cauliflower, carrots, celery, asparagus, turkey, chicken, winter squash, cantaloupe, eggplant, tomato, cabbage, grapes, pineapple, mushrooms, onions, oranges, plums, apples.

- **Iodine sources** – Cod, mackerel, yoghurt, spinach, seaweeds, kelp, turnip greens, garlic, watercress, pineapple, peas, artichoke, citrus fruits, egg yolks, lima beans, sunflower seeds.

- **High Antioxidant foods** – fresh fruit and vegetables – cranberries, blueberries, strawberries, mulberries. Richly coloured fruits and veggies contain flavonoids – blueberries, bilberries, broccoli, carrots, mangoes, spinach, cooked tomatoes, dark chocolate. These foods may help reduce free radicals in the body and prevent cell damage, thus reduce disease and cancer risk.

Sports Nutrition Physiology

Basic Exercise Physiology

There are two main types of energy regarding sports nutrition.

Chemical Energy: When our foods are broken down, this results in energy compounds being formed.

Mechanical Energy: Is used by the skeletal muscles as mechanical energy, from the result of the chemical compounds breaking down.

Adenosine triphosphate (ATP) is known as an energy rich molecule used during activity.

Energy for muscle contraction and activity is provided by the millions of ATP molecules stored in the muscle and broken down into adenosine diphosphate (ADP), that is one phosphate group is removed, and the energy is released. For the muscle to continue to contract, the ADP must be rebuilt to ATP.

A few seconds of exercise is all that the stored muscle ATP can handle. Therefore, the body requires other energy sources for more ATP to be formed, for further exercise or activity. This is due to Creatine Phosphate (CP) in the muscle being broken down to produce ATP, allowing a further 5-10 secs of exercise or activity.

When exercises requires more energy (ATP), other sources are used. Reserve fuels are also used such as carbohydrates and fats.

Energy Systems

The body generating energy is determined by the intensity and length of an activity.

Different exercises are divided into two main categories:

- Quick bursts of effort that need large amounts of energy over a short period of time. Eg. sprinting.
- Slower types of exercise that need energy continuously for a longer time.Eg. Cycling

Two different energy systems may be used during exercise or activity:

The Anaerobic System (without air)

- Is used for exercise or activity needing sudden bursts of energy. This energy system does not require oxygen to function. This energy comes from the muscles that contains phosphate Substances. This is called The Phosphate Energy System. or The Lactate Energy System may be used. This system relates to the formation of lactic acid, due to the sugars used in the muscle.

- The Phosphate Energy System – This occurs when CP is broken down, thus producing ATP. This provides fuel for 5-10secs of a maximum intensity. Eg.short sprints. The muscle can store CP in big amounts.

- Creatine Monohydrate (supplement): Supplies more CP, and thus allows for more reps.

- This system restores itself at 100% within 2 mins and 50% energy source is available after only 30 seconds of rest. If maximal effort is required for more than 8 seconds, an additional source of energy must be provided for the resynthesis of ATP. Food sources are used here.

- The Lactate Energy System – This energy system is used with very fast activity. Eg. Sprinting. Pyruvic acid results from the break down and then ATP energy. This replaces what the muscles have used. We call this glycolysis. This produces only 2 molecules of ATP, which makes it an in- efficient energy fuel. It is partly broken down with no oxygen required, and fully broken down with oxygen.

Lactic acid forms from the part break down. Lactic acid can become overloaded in the muscles when exercise is ongoing, and the body is unable to get rid of it fast enough, to the body producing it. This can cause muscle fatigue, which usually occurs in about 35 - 40 secs of very hard exercise. In 55 - 60 secs, exhaustion may result. To completely recover the body usually needs about 45 - 60 mins for the lactic acid to be gone.

This system is useful in a cross country event, for a quick finish. It gives us a fast amount of fuel for hard, small boosts of exercise.

The Aerobic System (with air)

This system is used when we need only a gradual stream of oxygen for our muscles to contract. Eg. Jogging.

This system is used at around medium intensity, and needs oxygen.

During increased exercise, with much oxygen needed, the fuel used, switches to glucose.

- Glucose molecules are broken down to create ATP via the Krebs (Citric Acid) Cycle and the Electron Transport Chain. This produces 34-36 molecules of ATP, much more than the anaerobic system with only 2 molecules of ATP produced.

- Aerobic energy is produced by carbohydrates and fats (minimally from amino acids) being broken down to form ATP. The process requires 20-25 chemical changes in the citric acid cycle and forms water and carbon dioxide.

This requires Nicotinamide adenine dinucletide (NAD - Vit B 3) and Flavin adenine dinucletide (FAD - Vit B2).

The aerobic system can provide large amounts of energy without forming lactic acid. Water is produced and CO_2 is expelled.

When a person becomes fitter, the cardiovascular system improves. Oxygen supplying the muscles. Therefore, there is an increase in oxygen used by the muscles during exercise.

We we call this "maximum oxygen uptake " (VO2 max). (ml / kg / min), or someone's aerobic capacity.

A higher VO2max allows the heart to pump blood to the lungs more effectively, and for oxygen to enter the muscles.

This system uses large muscles such as the trunk, thighs, shoulders, arms etc, with a heart rate over 120 beats per minute. Exercise is a minimum of 15 - 20 mins.

Sports Nutrition

For further information regarding sports nutrition or nutritional advice on general or specific health issues, please contact me for an appointment.

To further enhance your health and recovery, and get the most out of your exercise, contact me now for an individualised program to suit your needs. The program is tailor made based on your height, weight and exercise routine to suit each individual.

Hills Nutrition 4 Health

Website: www.hillsnutrition4health.com.au
Email: hillsnutrition4health@bigpond.com
Follow us on facebook and like. Look out for recipes, tips and useful information.

Sports Nutrition Treatment Plan

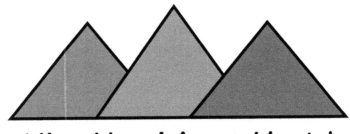

Hills Nutrition 4 Health
Personalised Nutritional Health Care

Sports Nutrition Treatment Plan

Date: _____

Name: _____
D.O.B: _____
Height: _____
Weight: _____

- To maintain Resting Metabolic Rate (RMR):_____ kcal/day required.
- Based on activity levels (_____ training, _____ days / wk): _____ kcal average / day required.

Training Days Food Intake

Daily Carbohydrate Intake: _____gms / kg body weight (_____gms Carbs / day, _____kcals)

Daily Protein Intake: _____gms / kg body weight (_____ gms Protein / day, _____kcals).

Daily Fat Intake:_____gms / kg body weight (_____ gms Fat / day,_____kcals).

Healthy Ratios in Sports

Carbs: 50-60%

Protein: 20-25%

Fats: 20-25% (Focus on good fats)

Pre-Exercise / Workout Meal Times

- 2-4 hrs before workout – Main Meal
- 1-2 hrs before workout – Snack or small meal
- Focus on Low GI options at this time

During Exercise / Workout

- When exercise is at high speed or training is longer than 1 ½ hrs, consider a 5-8% carb solution sports drink during training.
- 1gm carbs / kg body weight per hour of exercise
- Focus on High GI Carbs

Post Exercise / Training

- 4 to 1 Ratio Carbs to Protein especially in the first 4 hrs post exercise
- Start Carb/Protein intake within the first 30 mins post exercise.
- 1gm carbs / kg body weight, then 50gms carbs every 2hrs until the next main meal.

- 0.25gms Protein / kg body weight within 30 mins after training, and then approx. 15gms every 2hrs until the next main meal)
- Focus on High GI Carbs
- Vit C, E, Magnesium, Glutamine supplement reduces muscle damage and improves healing.

Pre-Workout Meal Ideas

2-4 hrs before exercise

- Sandwich/roll/wrap with chicken, fish, cheese, egg or peanut butter and salad or fruit
- Pasta with tomato based pasta sauce & cheese, and vegetables
- Spaghetti Bolognaise
- Baked potato with chicken, tuna, baked beans or cheese
- Chicken or prawn or tofu stirfry with noodles or rice
- Chicken with rice or quinoa and salad
- Crumpets with jam or nut butter & honey and flavoured milk
- Whole grain cereal (bran, muesli, wheat bix) / porridge with low-fat milk or yoghurt
- Fruit smoothies and / or energy bars

1-2 hrs before exercise

- Milk Shake or Fruit Smoothie
- Liquid meal replacement shake
- Sports bars / Cereal bars
- Fruit – bananas, apples, berries etc.
- Yoghurt
- Breakfast cereal with milk
- Dried apricots, dates or raisins
- Fruit loaf or raisin bread
- Muffins / crumpets / toast with jam or honey

During Exercise

- Isotonic Sports Drink (6gm/100ml) Eg. Gatorade: 30 gms Carbs / 500mls
- ½-1 energy bar: 30gms Carbs
- 1-2 bananas: 30gms Carbs

- Handful (40g) raisins or sultanas: 30gms Carbs
- 1 Cereal bar: 30gms Carbs
- Diluted fruit juice (1:1) 500mls: 30gms Carbs
- Energy Gel – 1 sachet: 30gms Carbs (1 cup water / ½ sachet, every 15-30 mins)
- Double or combine to give you 60gms Carbs

Post Workout Snacks

To be eaten within 30 mins to 2hrs after exercise and every 2hrs until next main meal

- Fruit Smoothe
- Protein / meal replacement shake
- 1-2 pieces of fruit with glass of milk
- 1-2 tubs yoghurt
- Homemade milkshake with fresh fruit or yoghurt
- Sports bar (Containing Carbs & Protein)
- Handful of dried fruit and nuts
- Sandwich/roll/wrap/bagel with lean protein (tuna, chicken, cottage cheese, peanut butter, egg)
- Bowl of whole grain cereal or porridge with milk
- Few rice cakes with jam or peanut butter and cottage cheese
- Baked potato with baked beans, tuna or cottage cheese

Sample: Daily Menu Plan (Provides approximately 530gms Carbs, 150gms Protein)

Breakfast

1 cup muesli with 200mls skim milk, 2 slices whole grain toast with 2 tbsp jam, 1 glass juice

Or

2 wholegrain toasted sandwiches with 2 poached or scrambled eggs and avocado

Lunch

2 bread rolls with 50gms chicken and salad, 1 banana, 1 fruit bun, 250ml flavoured low-fat milk
Or

1 large baked potato,100g cooked chicken, 1 bowl (125g) salad, 1 tbsp oil/vinegar dressing 1-2 pieces fruit (kiwi)

Dinner

Stirfry (with 2 cups pasta, 100gms meat, 1 cup vegetables) 1 piece fruit

Or

175g grilled salmon ½ plate (150g uncooked weight) brown rice 125g spinach or leafy green salad

During Workout or Sports

Isotonic Sports Drink (Gatorade)Alternate with water

Snacks & Post Workout

1 tub yoghurt & piece of fruit, or ,1 banana & handful of nuts (almonds, walnuts), or1 sports bar, or 600ml Sports Drink (Gatorade), or Banana & nut smoothie, or Handful of dried fruit (dates, apricots) & handful of nuts and seeds.

Fluid Intake

2-3 litres water daily

See your Nutritionist for an individualised sports nutrition program based on your activity & fitness. Please see a Nutritional pPractitioner for supplemental advice based on individual requirements.

Please note this information does not substitute for medical advice. Please see a medical or health practitioner if you suffer from a medical condition and or before starting a sports nutrition program.

Carbohydrate Foods

Food Ideas with 50gms Carbohydrates – low fat options

Bread and Cereals

- Bread – 4 slices
- Pocket bread – 2 small
- Pasta, cooked – 1 ¼ cups
- Brown rice, cooked – 1 cup
- Untoasted muesli – ¾ cup
- Weet-bix / vita brits – 5 biscuits
- All bran – 2 cups
- Oats, cooked – 2 ¼ cups
- Oats, raw – ¾ cup
- Lentils, cooked – 2 ½ cups
- Crumpets – 2 ½ average
- Muffins – 1 ½ average
- Wholemeal biscuits – 7
- Pancakes – 3
- Plain scones – 3 average
- Rice cakes - 5

Dairy Products

- Yoghurt (fruit) Skim – 400g
- Yoghurt (natural) skim – 800g

Vegetables

- Corn – 1 1/3 cups
- Potatoes – 2 medium
- Baked beans – 2 cups
- Broccoli – 20 cups

Fruit

- Apples / Oranges/Pears – 3 avg
- Apricots – 12
- Bananas – 2 medium
- Grapes – 45 medium
- Mangoes – 2 ½ medium
- Peaches – 9 medium
- Prunes – 15 average
- Strawberries – 12 cups
- Sultanas – 4 ½ tbsp.
- Watermelon – 5 ½ cups

Miscellaneous

- Muesli bars – 2 ½
- Jam – 3 tbsp
- Jelly beans – 50g packet
- Sports bars – 1 – 1 ½
- Fruit fingers – 3 ½
- Honey / Golden syrup – 2 tbsp
- Banana S/W – 2 slices bread, 1 banana

Protein Sources

FOOD	PORTION SIZE	PROTEIN (g)
Meat & Fish		
Beef, fillet steak, grilled, lean	2 slices 105g	31
Chicken breast, grilled	1 breast 130g	39
Turkey, light meat, roasted	2 slices 140g	47
Cod, poached	1 fillet 120g	25
Mackerel, grilled	1 fillet 150g	31
Tuna, canned in brine	1 small tin 100g	24
Dairy Products & Eggs		
Cheese, cheddar	1 thick slice 40g	10
Cottage cheese	1 small carton 112g	15
Skimmed milk	1 glass 200ml	7
Lowfat yoghurt, plain	1 carton 150g	8
Low-fat yoghurt, fruit	1 carton 150g	6
Eggs	1	8

Nuts & Seeds		
Peanut butter	On 1 slice bread 20g	5
Cashew nuts, roasted & salted	1 handful 50g	10
Walnuts	1 handful 50g	7
Sunflower seeds	2 tbsp 32g	6
Sesame seeds	2 tbsp 24g	4
Pulses		
Baked beans	1 small tin 205g	10
Red lentils, boiled	3 tbsp 120g	9
Red kidney beans, boiled	3 tbsp 120g	10
Chick peas, boiled	3 tbsp 140g	12
Soy Products		
Soy milk, plain	1 glass 200ml	6
Tofu	Half pack 100g	8
Grains & Cereals		
Wholemeal bread	2 slices 76g	6
Pasta, boiled	1 bowl 230g	7
Brown rice, boiled	1 bowl 180g	5

Contact Kathy

 (02) 9890 9213

www.hillsnutrition4health.com.au

Chapter Seven
Advanced Training

Featured Contributor - Garry Pedersen

About Garry Pedersen

Garry has been a qualified Squash Coach based in Victoria Australia for 33 years after reaching a high playing standard and being ranked in the top 100 players in the world, he now concentrates on Player development.

He is the founder of Squash Analysis. com which boasts 2500 players subscribed world wide and over 1400 videos on line.

Squash Analysis are now offering Coaching Camps as it is a great way to share the knowledge without regular weekly coaching.

Garry is a qualified coach and member of PSCAV. Garry managed to reach around 100 in the world standard while working a 40 hour per week job and running weekly coaching sessions in several different centres allowed Garry to develop the systems and methods that make such a huge difference to players he coaches today.

Coaching has always been a passion having coached at many clubs throughout Victoria, Australia and also in Linz, Austria, and Singapore.

The past 2 years Garry has been running regular camps for the Tasmanian State Junior Squad and concentrating on producing videos to give all players access to high-quality information without the high cost of personal coaching or the problems of access and availability of coaches.

You will walk away from a coaching session with Garry understanding the direction you need to go to improve your game. He has advanced hitting methods that see his coaching camps booked 12 months in advance.

What separates Garry from other coaches is the thousands of hours he has spent watching great players in slow motion on video, he is not only a trainer, he is a technique coach and can make a huge difference to your game in a short period of time.

Garry teaches how to use your Core muscles when hitting, how to keep the ball on the wall, how to kill the ball very short when Driving or even playing a Boast, the outcome will vary depending on the position of your body and the direction of your swing.

Much of what he teaches is minimal energy for amazing results in power and accuracy. A good example is that there is not one swing to hit a Forehand Drive we will show you 5 different swings all with different outcomes, when you understand them you then blend them to get the best outcome.

Garry explains the most joy he get is when he coaches players who have played for thirty plus years and within the first 30 minutes they become annoyed with a look of clarity and frustration at the same time, they realize they wish they had known this information on how to improve 20 years ago and wonder how good they could have been.

See why Garry's and squashanalysis.com's videos are the preferred source of Squash improvement videos in the world with proven technical methods that will greatly benefit coaches and players of all standards.

<u>Contact Garry</u>

✉ garry@squashanalysis.com

🌐 http://www.squashanalysis.com

ⓕ https://www.facebook.com/squashanalysis

SPECIAL OFFER

Email Garry and mention this book and you will get an extra 3 months membership on top of any other deal offered.

Advanced Squash Training

By Garry Pedersen

http://www.squashanalysis.com
https://www.facebook.com/squashanalysis

Win every match next season

We are going to give you the number one tip that will work in all situations no matter your standard or level of experience, there are limitations but if you apply this method you will be amazed at the results.

If you look at your current standard and the players you are playing and then make general observations on how often they play and train and secondly what type of training they are doing.

I am going to give you a snap shot of what I believe the average player today with a full time job, family and all the rest that goes with today's modern lifestyle.

Average Club player =

- Hits 3 times per week
- is active on non squash playing days
- Has a good diet trying not to eat too much fast food
- Does very little exercise for strength as all available time is taken with playing the game they love rather than going to the Gym.

So let's say you are serious about doing well next season, the answer is so simple I am sure you already know what comes next, you simply need to do more than your opponents. The good news is that the benchmark they have set is not too high and the room for improvement is vast.

If we start with the 3 hits per week - It may be difficult for you to get the time for more regular hits as most players lead a very busy life so the best option here is to run with a two pronged approach.

1. Increase the quality of your hits by actively seeking better players to hit with, it is very important that if you do this you treat them with respect for their game by not going for silly shots just to hopefully win points. Players love an opponent who applies themselves and structures rallies and has a purpose to what they are doing. When playing better players work on putting them in positions they cannot hurt you or connot hit winners from rather than trying to beat them with winners. This will make the rallies go longer, it will develop your court craft, and you will find yourself in great positions to attack off more often lessening the chance you will make errors when finishing rallies off.

2. Just before the start of the season or when you need to play well you need to find time to squeeze in an extra hit per week this only needs to be for a couple of weeks before you need to be playing well, this does amazing things for your game for a few reasons. If you played one more match per week you are increasing your court time by 25% increasing the familiarity with the court and motion of your body.

Your brain has the outcomes of each shot reinforced more often and your muscle strength for competitive match play is fine tuned, there is simply no better training for squash than playing as long as it is a quality match and not just going through the motions, so play keen motivated people and that is what you will get.

Next we look at diet, if you take a good look at what you eat remembering your body is like an engine and if you put poor quality fuel in it you will get a poor outcome in the form of energy and stamina. So not being qualified dietitian we will not say what you should be eating but rather set a goal for you to review what you eat and reduce the not so good food and increase the good quality food and your body and energy levels will increase accordingly.

Lastly we look at exercise, most people are lazy only doing what they have to for the results they achieve. It usually takes a few shock losses to inspire a player to do more and the first thing they do is to try and fit in another hit.

What if I said you could improve your game dramatically and it would barely affect your day to day lifestyle and cost you nothing. It is very simple and it is simply the most neglected area in squash, having and performing a daily exercise session is by far one of the easiest ways to improve your game and the good news if you are currently not doing it is that it will take very little time to get a great benefit both in your game and in your energy levels and how you feel about yourself.

The plan - The last thing you want to do is to get up early and set yourself an intense challenging workout, you will hate it and stop doing it in a few days and worse you will most likely never do it again. The answer is simple and you will be happy to do your workout every working day (weekends are for rest).

Firstly you need to form a routine, in other words get your body to crave or look for a workout at the same time each day, mornings are usually best as you get up earlier and will not be interrupted by unexpected developments any day can throw at you or even that just too tired feeling that gets us all some time.

The task - We are going to split your body into 3 areas, upper , core and lower and start with 2 exercises for each area. Here is the good bit, we are only going to ask you to do 10 of each and you are all done. This will take around 6 minutes of your day but remember we are not trying to make it hard so there will not be any heavy weights.

Suggestion - 10 Push ups, 10 Dips, 10 Leg raises, Planking for 30 seconds, 10 Squats and 10 Lunges.

The plan from here is that when you are ready, you increase the repetitions not the amount meaning you will do 2 sets of 10 and work toward 3 sets of 10. You can increase the numbers if you wish but try and not make it a chore to do, if you do not like a particular exercise don't do it, find another that works for the same muscle group and substitute it.

The last thing you need to understand is that you don't do push ups one day and get the reward the next day, real reward will come in around 30 days as long as you maintain the regularity. When you develop your exercise routine you may look to work upper body one session and lower body the next so you give your body time to recover but that is a fair way down the track.

This training will not affect your match in the evening so that is not a valid excuse to not do the work, it will however make you feel good about yourself as far as general health and strength and benefit you greatly regarding body strength allowing you to train harder during on court sessions.

Simulating Training

Prior to the modern shot players game of squash the main strategy was to rally the ball down the walls mostly and keep the ball tight, attacking shots would be played off shots that were loose.

This form of game structure saw the rallies 10, 20, 30 and even 40 or more shots in length. The game has changed with short bursts high energy which produces short, exciting rallies.

If we look at the time frames of old squash where a rally would last on average for 18 seconds and the players would have 6 seconds rest between points, today the game has evolved to 8 second rallies and 6 seconds rest.

The shorter rallies are allowing players to work harder and be more dynamic with their movement and stroke play.

So clever players have developed their training to simulate the efforts required in a game, there is little need to hit the track for a one hour run when other than the cardio benefit it will work against you slowing your motion down and there is always the relentless impact of hard road surfaces to consider, the answer is to replicate what you do in a game on the training track.

The breakdown of a typical match is 15 second rallies, 6 seconds rest which makes most games go for around 5 to 10 minutes depending on if it is a one sided match or a close match.

Every 10 minutes you can have a 90 second break to simulate the break between games. So now we have our training parameters and if we factor in that we want to be better than anyone else we go for the high side of the work required so we are ready for anything.

Simulated training = 15 seconds work 6 seconds rest for 10 minutes and build up to repeat for 5 repetitions (5 games) with 90 seconds between each set.

That brings us to work rate or intensity and this is what separates good and awesome, it is one thing to train but another to push yourself striving to improve your strength, balance under motion and your recovery.

Top players learn how to train with intensity and take the advantage of hard work on to the court with them so when the game gets tough, they are looking for more and not to play do or die shots to control energy use.

Ghosting

Ghosting is movement around the court without a ball swinging and playing shots as though there was a ball to be hit. The main benefit is that you can practice balanced movement and increase the speed and strength in your body without having to control the ball.

Ghosting plays a critical part in all great players training, if you practice controlled movement it will become second nature and done without thinking in a match.

Watch high level players and they will look like they are not running at all seeming to float across the court, this is practiced on the court without a ball so there are no adjustments to be made to suit the pace of the ball or the variation in height.

You must clearly understand the movement methods before starting to train this way with careful thought given to body and racquet preparation as you approach to play a shot, his will increase the options you have when you are playing a real match.

There are many different theories on the best movement so do your research and work out your preferred method and then use ghosting to become proficient at it.

I believe there are several key things to work on with coming out of your shot being just as important as approaching the ball. The movement to the ball can be broken down to two different movements, one for when you need to move a long way and another for short moves.

Longer distances such as moving from the back of the court to the front of the court should be performed by using as large controlled steps as possible, this allows you to be low on final step and with less forward motion over your front leg meaning your skeleton will stop some of your forward motion on your final step rather than your muscles doing all the work.

Shorter moves should be done with a shuffle move as it is extremely fast and requires less body turn keeping your head very well balanced and is very quick to recover from. This is the movement that makes great players look as they are in full control.

No matter which shot you play you should always come out of your shot with a shuffle which is a very quick movement and allows easy body turn when you choose to change direction to go for the next shot, you do however usually only shuffle once then step toward the T timing your movement to be in the centre of the court just as your opponent strikes his shot.

There are great movement patterns to be practiced when ghosting and if you time your patterns you will enjoy the challenge improving your court coverage. A lot of this type of training comes down to your ability to recover and do the next set at top pace within a set time frame at all times controlling your balance. Top players learn to love this kind of training to the point where it becomes just a training session rather than a physical challenge but for Club standard players just 5 minutes every now and then will greatly improve your court coverage.

Volley is the key

Ask any top level player and they will tell you they just need to volley more with quality which will allow them to reduce the time for their opponent to get in a good position and open up winner opportunities if played well, tThis is much easier than it sounds but there is a method to achieve this.

There are two components to this, firstly the movement to get you in a balanced position and secondly the ability to execute the shot.

If we take a look at the movement you will find you are probably making the same mistake 90% of players are making and that is that you are trying to cover the down the wall drive from the T or centre of the court. this is too far away from the side wall as proven by taking the quickest move you can allowing two steps or a quick shuffle there will still be around 30 centimeters of one foot in length from your racquet to the side wall, even if you could reach the side wall you can only reach the wall at hip height leaving you vulnerable higher and lower as this requires extra reach.

The answer is simple, if the player striking is in the back Forehand corner you move in toward the side wall about half way between the centre and the service box, assuming your shot is near the side wall then your opponent will still have the whole front wall to hit to if they choose. If your opponent hits a cross court you have longer to turn and get the shot so this is not a problem.

The second part is the execution of the shot, as long as you have made a balanced approach with minimal backswing you will be able to deflect the shot rather than have a full swing giving you full control over the front of the court. if you need to hit deeper simply hold your muscles stronger, keep your volley mid height just hitting upward landing the ball in the target zone just behind the service box.

No matter what training you are doing you need to simulate the time frames of your match and with most rallies being around 20 seconds the good news is that you keep your work to that time. Between points is around 10 seconds so that is the amount of rest you have before starting your next 20 seconds of work.

On average a game will last around 10 minutes and so the formula for your training becomes 20 seconds work with 10 seconds rest for 10 minutes.

If you do this for 5 rotations as though you were playing a 5 set match, you will be fully prepared for anything.

It is one thing to set time frames around your training but the true competitive athlete will maintain the intensity and this is where most fail. I suggest you keep the resistance, weight or distance on an easy level and concentrate on keeping the intensity high to maintain fast balanced motion and then build up as you get stronger and fitter.

This means if you are riding a bike you keep it easy and fast or running without changing directions then build to shuttle runs or court sprints and then adding short distance with many change of directions, intensity is critical to get the most out of your session.

Better players volley more which gives their opponent less time to regain balance and make a good position to return your shot it also means that you do not need to go to the back corners to retrieve the ball and therefore less movement. If you analyze the movement you will notice there is less running and more leg and lower body strength required and very fast speed to get in a good position to volley.

If we agree that it is better to Volley more then you need to train your body to move in a way that you can quickly cover the court, the answer it to develop your shuffle muscles. If you were to face the front wall and cover the sides of the court like a soccer goalie you will become very quick and maintain balance and as the Volley requires very little preparation your options are good for a range of shots.

For any type of volley the best way to approach is to keep your hips open to the front wall giving you full reach on the forehand side and a full range of shot options, today's racquets are so powerful that with almost no backswing you can put the ball down the back with quality and quite hard.

 Limiting your swing will also reduce the movement of the racquet and therefore limit the chance of making an error with all movement fully controlled and strong.

If you choose to play a Drop Volley the amount of swing required is minimal with the top players today choosing to deflect the ball rather than hit to the front corners, this has the added advantage of taking the pace off the ball and finishing very short.

Squash like few other games can be practiced by yourself and the amount of individual Volley routines available to you mean you will not get bored, video web sites such as squashanalysis.com not only show you the routine but explain the key ways to improve your consistency and quality.

Remember if you have bad habits and you repetitively practice you are cementing bad habits, just one change in the direction you swing your racquet can have an amazing result on the outcome of your shots and the enjoyment of the game.

Targets

Better players hit Targets more often and at the top level, it is when a player misses Target they open the court for their opponent to attack. The first thing you do is to clearly understand where your Targets are.

For a Drive target you do not aim for a spot on the front wall as this depends on how hard you hit the ball, you aim where you want the ball to bounce on the floor after hitting the front wall. You need the ball to be traveling downward toward the back wall so it does not jump up and come out after it hits the back wall. For a straight Drive the Target is just behind the service box and within four floorboards of the side wall.

When playing a Cross court Drive the target is the same depth but to just hit the side wall as low as possible so it bounces twice quickly binding the ball in the back corner.

There is a second target when cross courting if your opponent starts to intercept and volley your cross court, when this happens adjust your target to hit the side wall level with them making it difficult to get a clean volley, in this case you are not worried about where the ball goes after it gets past the player and it is better to hit the side wall even just before them to compensate for the player reaching forward.

Boast targets are often miss understood with many players smashing the ball into the side wall to get it across to the other wall. For a Boast you want the ball to bounce twice just after hitting the front wall and before the second side wall, if the ball hits the second side wall it will come back in toward the centre of the court.

When playing a Lob you do not aim to hit the side wall at all or you will risk hitting out of court, it is far better to hit as high as you can in the middle back of the court so the ball comes down on your opponent and not toward them this will often take them off balance and make it very difficult to play a quality shot often setting you up for an easy shot for a winner.

There are two different targets for Drops, if the ball is wider than the service box you can aim for the nick so the ball rolls out but if the ball is closer to the side wall you should aim to hit the front wall then floor so the ball continues to go into the side wall and further away from your opponent and hopefully on the wall when they want to hit it.

When serving it is very important to hit the side wall before your opponent can hit the ball, it does not matter how hard you hit the side wall should take away the chance for a winner to be played off your serve.

Deep Volleys use the same targets as Drives and short volleys are the same targets as Drops.

The height and pace you hit the volley become more important for control which will enable you to hit target, try not to lob your volley and go with a solid direct hit to target when volleying.

Planning your Improvement

There is a method that will amaze you and bring great benefit to your game but for this to be truly successful you must be very honest with yourself.

I am going to ask you to evaluate yourself for the main areas of Squash in order to identify your weaknesses and give you an improvement plan, give yourself a score with 1 being not good and 10 being exceptional.

Here are the skills:

- Racquet ability
- Fitness
- Strength
- Speed
- Agility / Flexibility
- Shot Consistency
- Power
- Court movement
- Concentration
- Game Plan

If you scored lower than 7 for any of these skills then you need to develop a plan to improve these areas. You need to write down the steps required to get you to the skill level you require and set short term and long term goals.

Long term goals are to say that in 6 months you need to be able to run a certain distance or to lift a certain weight or play a set up shot and reduce your error rate dramatically, your short term goals are what you are going to do this week to help achieve your long term goal.

If you find you do not move around the court well you can set a test and time yourself on a skill like a 6 point movement without a ball having 60 swings, with this as a bench mark you then need to do some research and find the best way to move so you practice good habits and then set a plan to do 5 minutes of this court movement work at least 3 times per week but preferably more and you will build the muscles and control required.

Every month you can take the test again to monitor your improvement. You will be amazed at just how easy it is if you focus on a task to improve a specific area.

The quality of information you get to decide on the technique you will use to improve your outcome makes all the difference so you should go to reputable web sites like squashanalysis.com or you will be merely practicing bad habits. Technique can also reduce the amount of energy required to perform a task as well as improve outcomes

Regardless of your strengths and weaknesses there is on an area that will always improve your game, Strength and conditioning. When you think of training at the top level, you tend to think of players hitting thousands of balls but in reality the biggest advancements in your game will come from strength and conditioning. This is also the area you have greatest control over, it much harder to develop your racquet skills and much easier to develop your fitness.

Most people think of strength and think of power hitting and aggressive body drive through the ball where in reality the real benefit is in the quick early take off and streamlined movement getting rid of all excess movement and hitting strongly with an efficient swing.

Without strength players rely on flick and excessive turn to get an outcome and usually have that relentless just in control feeling with moderate outcomes leaving themselves open to a quality game as they scramble to make good court position.

It is also very important to work on the strength component of your game so you can approach your shot with full body control allowing preparation and this is what makes racquet ability work for you, being in a good position early is the key to shot quality and shot options.

You can develop a method of measuring all skills and this will give you a clear understanding of your rate of improvement, measuring your outcomes will tell you exactly your progress rather than just feeling you are getting better. Develop a test and revisit the same exercise over time.

Game Plan

Next you need to understand your own game and play a style of game that compliments your strongest game style. Are you a

- Power hitter
- Lob and Dropper
- Full attack player
- Counter punch hitter
- Relentless quality hitter
- Run your opponent into the ground with your fitness

Your aim is to make sure you are playing your game style and not following your opponents style of play, people often get caught in a power hitting struggle with the outcome being poor quality targets and few winners, few players can hit relentless quality at full pace.

Tempo or the time between each hit is very important, you will have an ideal tempo where you move at a controlled pace and hit at a controlled pace while maintaining an attacking game.

You will find that if you are continually rushed you cannot settle into a rhythm which leads you into going for shots when you are not ready or poor shot choice off a bad body position.

To take this one step further if you understand or can identify your opponent's desired rhythm and not allow them to become comfortable with the game tempo then you will make it harder for them to concentrate, this often requires change of pace and varying shot selection.

If we look at a typical match, this is how you should approach the early stages of the first game. Play your desired tempo and style of play, you should get a feeling of weather you are likely to win with this plan toward the end of the game, if you are winning work on maintaining the intensity and quality and do not change your game to win faster just enjoy the feeling of being in control. If you are losing and feel you rarely controlled the rallies you need to change your game plan.

If you are struggling there are several options and all will have the same desired outcome which is to change the rhythm or tempo of the game. You can lift the ball up to get the ball to the back rather than the power

Drive which will make your opponent have to do more work to maintain the tempo, this is often good even when you are stable and have options allowing you to maintain a good court position and feel in control for a few shots, but you must still hit Target or keep the ball tight for this to work.

Another option is to play more moving shots such as Boasts and Drops, this will change the flow of the game quickly but also means you will need to do plenty of work.
If you choose to open up the game with shots, you must realize the short shots are only good after you have pushed your opponent deep or the occasional

Volley Drop from a good body position. A short swing should improve your consistency and requires little follow through keeping you stable and balanced to cover the court.

Another great way to change a match is to make sure you are always in front of your opponent on the court and not cutting behind them to get deep shots, you will start to drive deeper and move forward allowing you to cover short shots when they are played.

This gives a feeling of dominating your opponent and controlling the rally even though you are not hitting winners.

From the front, you can lob them back to keep them back and reduce the chance of them playing a volley winner. This should be practiced as part of your normal game as it is one of the best ways to fully control a game.

If you find yourself in a situation where you are well down in a game there is a way to change the flow of the game and it often has amazing results. If you work on moving your opponent around the court with no winners and the sole purpose becoming to tire them out for the next game the whole game changes, you will make less errors and often they just want to finish the game and rush into attacking shots and make errors.

Forget about the score completely and solely concentrate on the rally you are playing , I have often found myself checking the score to find I am back in the game that I previously had no hope of winning. If you lose the game as expected hopefully your opponent is tired and will struggle in the next game.

All of these game plan suggestions will only have an impact if you are reasonably close in standard to your opponent they will not allow you to beat someone who is much stronger or a higher grade, to beat much better players you need to develop your fundamentals and improve consistency under stress and that is part of the fun of Squash.

The best thing I can suggest to you to develop your game is to realize that you can always learn, try not to become too technically perfect and have some individualism in the way you play some shots.

Watch others and understand why they are playing certain shots and have a plan for your improvement.

Squash is no different to anything else in life, if you work on a system of continual improvement you will find you are happy with your game.

Chapter Eight

World Squash
Player Journey

Featured Contributor - Steve Walton

I am the Director of Inform Connection which is the largest Squash business in the Southern hemisphere. We distribute Grays, Hi-tec, Salming and Dunlop Squash Equipment to Squash businesses Australia wide.

With these brands we sponsor over 100 Australian athletes and 200 Australian events, returning $250,000 through these avenues per annum.

Inform Connection also owns www. squash.com.au one of the worlds largest Squash Retail Businesses with over 15 stores around Australia and a central website. All profits are shared with the Squash Centre partners 50:50.

In addition I am the Founder of Squash United and a consultant to www.squashanalysis.com and The Squash Mechanics.

Steve Walton like many players got involved in squash when he was growing up. He started in Australia and and and played in World Squash Championships and acheived a top 100 world ranking. He shares his story about how he started and his journey world ranking and back.

Steve owns and operates Inform Connection, which has been operating in Australia since 1996 and has developed a wide range of squash programs and services.

The Inform Circuit includes both Open and Junior Graded events catering for all standards and ages.

Inform Connection is the International Brand Managers for Grays Squash, National Distributors for i-Max Protective Eyewear, Hi-Tec Shoes and Squash Design Shoes.

His main focus includes:

- Junior Squash Events
- Open Squash Events
- Squash Trainer
- Racquetball
- Squash Design
- Special Squash Events

Contact Steve

 07 5445 3733

 www.informconnection.com.au

Journey to become a World Squash Player

Steve Walton grew up in Melbourne and regularly played AFL. One day he had got an ingrown toenail and couldn't get footy boots on. His father had the weekly squash booking, and he said, "Steve why don't you come down to squash club and run around a bit and it will keep you fit."

So Steve went down to the squash court and had his first game. Steve took the game very quickly and started to playing with other juniors at the club. He was lucky because the club had lots of juniors to compete with and improve his match skills.

Steve started winning all the competitions, then went onto tournaments, which got him a good state ranking. He then found a good coach. Pretty soon he was playing seven days a week. In fact, it was his addiction to squash that lead him to the courses he studied at the university.

One day he was sitting around the table with his mates at High School and was everyone saying what they were going to do next year, and Steve said, "Well I'm going to be a physical education teacher, that way I can stay fit."

He kept his word and enrolled into a PE course and kept squash training at an intense level. He got even fitter because of the whole PE side of things. He even lectured the squash unit at the end of the course because the lecturer realized that he knew more than the teacher.

When Steve completed university, he moved to Geelong and, luckily, he ended up sharing accommodation with someone who had just returned from playing professional squash overseas. They started to train together and got him to a level where he could have a crack at pro-coaching.

Steve had a slight interruption along the way. One day on his way to the university, he had a head-on car accident at 100 km an hour and smashed his leg badly. This meant his dream to become a pro-coach was on hold for around a year. It made him hungry to quickly get back into squash, and because of his PE training, he had to rebuild his training and get his fitness and skill levels back.

Steve became a pro-coach and taught for several years which lead him to move to London. He also went to Vancouver, Canada, ran a bed & breakfast there in return for free food and accommodation. While he was training, he was introduced to the World Squash Women's team. He then moved to New York managed a hostel there.

He moved back to London which is where he still is, the epicentre of high-level squash. He started to play in some leagues and clubs.

Steve was able to start training with some very good players. He started helping out and managing a player by the name of Matt Crawker, who was ranked in the top 40 in the world at the time.

Steve then started traveling around playing the pro events, especially in Europe, because there are lots of them in Europe. He was also able to play in Japan

Then he met a girl, Lisa, who he ended up marrying.

He was managing a teaching agency while He was in London to make money because it's difficult to make a living out of just playing squash even at a high level.

Steve went to play the British Open, which was in Wales, in Cardiff, and at the competition met a Portuguese player called Louis Balbosa. The President of the Portuguese Squash Association.

They got chatting in the change room about what squash is like in Portugal. Steve didn't know much about it; he had been to Portugal.

Through that conversation, they said, "Oh look, would you like to come and help us train the squad?" Steve said, "Oh yeah, that'd be interesting."

Steve discovered just how corrupt squash associations could be in some of the fringe European countries. During his time there he ended up growing into becoming the national squash coach for Portugal,

Steve continued to play in squash events and was able to get this ranking into the top 100. But at this time he was enjoying coaching more than all the playing. Every time he went to play it cost him money. Even when you won the event, the prize money was not enough to cover the airfares and accommodations.

It was while he was there that he and his wife, Lisa, started importing squash racquets from England and everywhere else because no one in Portugal could get racquets.

One of the racquet brands he started importing was Grays. The Managing Director of Grays, Richard Gray, rang him one dayand said, "Just wanted to know who you are and what you're doing and how is it you selling more Grays racquets in Portugal than we're selling through most of Europe."
Steve had also started running tournament and competitions in Portugal and in Spain. They were distributing Karakal's.

Then unfortunately, they received a call that Lisa's father had a heart attack and because of their concern over his health they decided to move back to Australia

They already had a business in Portugal called InForm Sport so Inform Connection was born in Australia.

Steve was also now managing some Australian players. He started managing Paul Price who achieved a ranking of number four in the world.
Also John Williams who was ranked in the top ten, and Glen Kane who got top fifty. They also started running regular weekend tournaments.

They ended running almost fifty events a year. Some weekends they had more than one event on.

One day he looked at his calendar and we had a completely blank weekend. He said to himself, "How did this happen?" So he scheduled an event for it.

When he came home and told Lisa, who gave him one of those looks like you've done something horribly wrong but he never knew what it was. That was the weekend they were getting married!

So he quickly cancelled that event. The court owner still laughs at him about it to this day because he couldn't believe Steve had stayed unmarried for so long.

Steve to this day is still doing all the tournaments in Australia and distributing Grays and then sponsoring a lot of players.

He has built up a solid network and also now distributes Hi-Tec brands as well.

Steve then started the business name squash.com.au and signed retail partnerships around Australia. They give 50% of all the profits back to the stores whereas every other online sales company just keeps it all.

He does it this way because he wants to keep squash courts open.

They now also distribute Salming, which is the fastest growing squash brand in the world. Steve still plays the occasional tournament including Jumbo Doubles squash event in Singapore as well as Masters events every now and again.

Steve believes Squash is running at different paces everywhere in the world. Squash in Australia and in the UK seems like it will continue to stay in decline.

It's partly because many squash centers are closing down. A lot of squash centers are on prime real estate. Whereas in other countries in the world, other Asian countries and some Eastern European countries they are new to the game. They're building facilities that are not stand-alone Squash centers.

The concept of new squash centres is being part of that health hub. It which is far more sustainable. That means the owners or the consortium is not just relying on people getting on the squash court.

Steve thinks the next challenge to squash to Australia is to build sustainable squash centers. Either following a 24-7 model which means they can be largely unmanned or only manned at this peak times.

Like a 24-7 gym.

There's real scope there. There's certainly some people working towards that. Greg Tilton in Sydney is already operating a 24-7 squash center.

He's proven it can be done. He built it on an industrial estate.

The challenge always for squash associations everywhere is they're always scrambling for money. Squash in Australia has lost a lot of money from the Australian Sorts Commission so they're looking into developing new pathways.

Steve doesn't think there's one answer on how squash is going. In some parts of the world, squash is booming. In Egypt they have managed to get four or five people in the top ten in men's and a few in the women's rankings.

They're queuing up at the doors to get on the squash court there. Whilst Egypt was involved in squash for a long time, this is the first time they've been dominant, so it's growing there.

In Australia, the biggest problem is because we play a lot of outdoor sports. In England, the weather's not very good usually and in those Middle Eastern countries, it's quite hot outside.

As an indoor sport, it's more desirable than in Australia where they want to go to the beach or they want to go play some sort of outdoor sport.

The options for people in Australia in a sporting sense are phenomenal. Squash really doesn't have much marketing in Australia.

Other than every four years when the Commonwealth Games is on, squash doesn't get a lot of air time.

The squash buildings from the outside are not incredibly obvious about what's in them.

It's a bit strange place. They could be in basements or something.

They look a bit intimidating. You drive past a tennis court; it's pretty obviously what it's for -- football or cricket field. Squash it's just a big block, so people don't really know what's going on there.

He doesn't think squash will ever be back to the booming as it was in the 70's, but it can certainly be back bigger than what it is right now. It just needs some sustained effort.

If you look at soccer when Australia got a team in the finals or got fairly high ranked there; soccer took off in Australia because of all the young kids wanted to play it. If you got lucky and got squash into the Olympics or something like that, then we might have a chance of being able to get that awareness.

When Steve was at the Commonwealth Games in Glasgow and commented that it was the best squash he had ever been to.

It was a purpose-built temporary building, and the court was fantastic. The place was absolutely packed. Squash can be put on very cheaply compared to some other sports.

Sure and it's a high impact game where there's a lot of action going. Like tennis can drag it out, whereas squash is very intense and it's very action-packed.

Once people understand it, squash is a fantastic bang for your buck. The biggest challenge it would have is if people aren't familiar with the game, they might not appreciate some of the great skill that's on the show.

Again with the high definition cameras and all equipment that's available now, Squash could fit quite well for television.

Squash Federation and the Professional Squash Association have done fabulous work in the last five years in packaging. There's now quite a bit of content readily available or subscription available.

There's has been a lot of changes to the squash courts in recent years and to the visibility through the glass for cameras.

A lot of the general population would be amazed if they saw a four-wall glass court and a colored floor. Steve has seen a lot of portable courts at major events like Boston and Egypt.

Nearly every major championship is on a portable four-wall glass court that's either in Grand Central, in New York or the one that was just in Hong Kong or the Shanghai one. Nearly all of them are like that now. So that's the future of the game. The reason is it takes the game to the people.

Rather than the other way around here, you can increase your audience then because you can have people all around that. Whereas before you'd have a small amount of people at the back. They're sometimes looking over the top of the brick walls.

Exactly, so those days are definitely gone. All major tournaments are on four-wall glass courts now. The players get quite upset if they have to play a qualifying match on a hard court. The ball does bounce differently and the sound is very different. The sound of the glass compared to the sound of concrete is quite different.

On the subject of the building of new squash courts, there are more people here qualified to build squash courts now than what he has ever seen before.

Sarah Fitzgerald and her husband Cam, hold the Australian rights to CourtTech, and they built the courts up in Darwin. They built the courts in Next Gen in Canberra.

Also Rodney Martin has the rights to McGill, and they have built some squash courts.

Contact Steve

 07 5445 3733

 www.informconnection.com.au

Chapter Nine
Wrapping Up

Wrapping Up
"Game Over"

We hope you have enjoyed The Game of Squash. Our aim was to provide new and advanced players an interesting and useful guide to one of the oldest and enjoyable sports in the world.

If you can improve your squash skills, this will lead to more challenging games and the payoff in fitness and general health.

If you new to squash, we hope we have inspired a visit to your local club. If you are already playing, consider some of our ideas to improve your game and win more matches!

We have a website that you can visit to get more information and access to any extra bonuses we provide. www.thegameofsquash.com

We also have Facebook and Twitter if you want to engage with us on social media.

If you are in Sydney check out www.squashmate.com.au and we look forward to seeing you at Baulkham Hills Squash and Fitness!

Lightning Source UK Ltd.
Milton Keynes UK
UKOW06f1955050517
300618UK00007B/377/P